THE LITTLE BOOK OF

COLLEGE FOOTBALL LAW

CECIL C. KUHNE III

AMERICAN BAR ASSOCIATION
Defending Liberty
Pursuing Justice

Cover design by Andrew Alcala/ABA Publishing.

Printed in the United States of America.

18 17 16 15 14 5 4 3 2 1

Library of Congress Cataloging-in-Publication Data

Kuhne, Cecil C., III, 1952-
 Little book of college football law / Cecil C. Kuhne III.
   pages cm
 Includes bibliographical references and index.
 ISBN 978-1-62722-833-6 (alk. paper)
 1. College sports—Law and legislation—United States. 2.
Football—Law and legislation—United States. 3. College
athletes—Legal status, laws, etc.—United States. 4. School
sports—Law and legislation—United States. 5. College sports—Law and
legislation—United States—Cases. 6. Football—Law and
legislation—United States—Cases. 7. National Collegiate Athletic
Association. I. Title.
 KF4166.K84 2014
 344.73'099—dc23   2014032534

Discounts are available for books ordered in bulk. Special consideration is given to state bars, CLE programs, and other bar-related organizations. Inquire at Book Publishing, ABA Publishing, American Bar Association, 321 N. Clark Street, Chicago, Illinois 60654-7598.

www.ShopABA.org

Table of Contents

Introduction

For most of us football fans, it isn't too difficult to conjure up vivid memories of a pleasant fall afternoon on our favorite college campus—briskly and enthusiastically approaching the football stadium, proudly clad in our team's colors, surrounded by the excited throng of fans, the crisp air reverberating from the blare of the school's fight song. Whether we graduated last year or decades ago, that compelling anticipation doesn't seem to dissipate much with the passage of time.

In other words, college football is timeless.

And so, it seems, are the controversies that surround this traditional and nostalgic endeavor filled with more than its fair share of passionate people—the players, the coaches, the spectators, and even the National Collegiate Athletic Association (NCAA). The result is a fascinating body of law that has developed around one of the country's most popular sports, delving into areas you probably never imagined.

* * *

First of all, a plethora of lawsuits deal with the players themselves, presenting such intriguing issues as the following:

- Does a university owe a football player who is prone to back injury a *special* duty of care based upon his status as an athlete?
- Is a university liable for gender discrimination when it dismisses a female field goal kicker because of the unfavorable media publicity she creates for an otherwise all-male team?
- Can a football player who was disqualified for medical reasons by the team physician force the university to reinstate

him if he provides a release of liability and clearance from other physicians?

- Is a football player entitled to workers' compensation for an injury sustained on the field?
- What steps must a sports publisher take to secure adequate permission to use an athlete's photograph in a well-publicized advertising program?

∗ ∗ ∗

And there is captivating litigation dealing with college football coaches, such as these issues:

- Can the university dismiss an assistant football coach for an arrest related to public drunkenness without violating his rights as a statutorily protected "disabled person"?
- Is a coach who leaves to take another job liable to the university for reciprocal (and substantial) liquidated damages provisions under his employment agreement?
- Can a coach who is fired bring a defamation action against the university for statements contained in an unflattering newspaper article and for remarks made at a meeting with the parents of the team members?
- Can a terminated coach sue the university president and athletic director for failing to mention that the employment contract he signed is unenforceable under the doctrine of sovereign immunity?
- Must a university, when lawfully terminating its head coach under the provisions of an employment contract, continue to pay for job-related fringe benefits such as the services of an administrative assistant and travel to football clinics?

* * *

And then there is a range of lawsuits brought by the spectators, posing such interesting legal conflicts as these:

- Can a drunken student at a football game, who vaulted over a wall and fell 30 feet into the concrete stands, sue the university for *not* protecting "a person in plaintiff's inebriated condition" from injury?
- Does a university have an obligation to protect fans in the end zone from injury by those who lunge wildly for errant footballs?
- Can a spectator who is injured while hanging from a goal post after celebrating a game bring an action against the university for damages sustained in such post-game revelry?
- Is a private university *exempt* from liability as a charity when the personal injury occurs to a business invitee at a football game who does not allege negligent hiring of the university's employees?

* * *

And last, but certainly not least, a number of thought-provoking decisions deal with the various rules promulgated by the NCAA:

- Do NCAA sanctions violate players' "constitutionally protected rights" to participate in intercollegiate athletic competitions?
- Can a university bring an anticompetition and price-fixing action against the NCAA for limiting the number of televised games it can broadcast?

- Do the NCAA no-draft and no-agent rules violate antitrust laws by restricting opportunities in the labor market for college football players?
- Are NCAA rules that limit the size of advertising logos permitted on athletes' uniforms in violation of the Sherman Act?

* * *

In your hands is a riveting and amusing collection of sports jurisprudence dealing with a number of major collegiate football programs from around the country. You now have but one option available—to lie back and dream of autumn and another football season yet to come.

THE LITTLE BOOK OF

COLLEGE FOOTBALL LAW

PART I

PLAYERS

Chapter One

Pain in the Back: Defining the Duty of Care

Orr v. Brigham Young University, 108 F.3d 1388 (10th Cir. 1977)

One morning during fall practice, a Brigham Young University football player named Vernon Orr felt pain in his back after a rigorous workout with a blocking sled. He was immediately sent to the head trainer, who speculated that Orr had immobilized his sacroiliac joint (the one located between the spine and the pelvis). The injury was promptly treated with heat, massage, and electric stimulation.

As a result of his incapacitation, Orr missed practice that afternoon, and the coach allegedly berated him for doing so. Orr spoke with the trainer the next morning, and as practice proceeded, his condition gradually improved. Later that day, the coach instructed Orr to keep seeing the trainer. He did so—he received five or six more treatments—and then he stopped. About six weeks later, he experienced another episode and was once again sent to the trainer. The pain, fortunately, resolved itself, and Orr had no further problems.

The following spring, Orr once again suffered a gradual onset of lower back pain and stiffness. He sought therapy, which was successful. The next fall, the coach asked him about his back, and he responded, "It's not too bad yet." The coach recommended that Orr start seeing the trainer, but he never followed up. During the last game of the year, Orr complained of back pain at half-time, and he was examined by two orthopedic specialists. The doctors found no sign of disc or neurological impairment, and Orr returned to the field with explicit instructions that he was to leave *immediately* if the pain increased or changed. After the game, all players who had been injured were instructed to report to the clinic the next day, but Orr declined to do so.

During practice two weeks later, Orr suffered yet another back injury. He was referred to the medical staff. Examination revealed reticular pain, and an x-ray showed three herniated discs. He was immediately referred to a neurological surgeon, who performed surgical repair. At the end of the semester, Orr abruptly left school to play professional football in Finland.

Remarkably enough, Orr filed suit against BYU, and in his complaint he alleged that the coaches and trainers failed to provide adequate medical care for his series of back injuries. He also claimed that the coaching staff placed enormous pressure on him to continue playing while he was hurt.

Orr advanced several theories of negligence. He argued that BYU owed him a duty of care based upon a "special relationship" created by his status as an athlete; that the university created a situation in which playing him would cause him harm, thus imposing an affirmative duty to protect him from injury; that the university allowed its trainers to practice medicine without a license; and that the university breached its duty of care in the diagnosis and treatment of his injuries.

Orr specifically alleged that BYU breached its duty of care in the following respects:

- Engendering a win-at-all-costs mentality,
- Excessively pressuring players to perform,
- Using psychological pressure to achieve performance at the expense of his health,
- Creating disincentives to report injuries or seek medical attention,
- Employing unqualified personnel to diagnose and treat injuries,
- Misdiagnosing his injuries,
- Failing to have the trainers refer him to a team physician for diagnosis and treatment,
- Failing to hire a full-time team physician responsible for diagnoses and treatment in lieu of unqualified trainers,
- Encouraging him to play after being injured,
- Using pain-killing injections to enable him to continue to play without completely diagnosing his injury,
- Placing greater emphasis on winning games than on his physical and mental health, and
- Engaging in the unauthorized practice of medicine.

BYU responded that—with the exception of medical negligence—the duties it allegedly breached were not ones that had ever been recognized by the Utah courts.

Orr persisted in his theory of a special relationship between a university and its athletes that was above and beyond that owed to students in general. Orr urged that by recruiting him to play football, BYU assumed responsibility for his safety and deprived him of the norm-al opportunity for self-protection. He asserted that the university had a *special* duty to protect his physical well-being by *not* playing him when doing so would exacerbate his injury.

In reviewing the case, the Tenth Circuit concluded that the Utah Supreme Court had previously held that a university had only an educational—rather than a custodial—relationship with its students. The court could not find a single state case recognizing a unique relationship between a university and its student-athletes, and it was understandably reluctant to alter state law in the absence of clear guidance from Utah's highest court.

The appellate court did concede that as a football player Orr had certain demands placed upon him that were different than those of the average college student. But those distinctions were more of a contractual nature, since BYU had agreed to provide its student-athletes with such benefits as financial assistance, meals, training equipment, medical services, and academic support. The court agreed that medical services negligently performed could result in liability, but it found nothing in the facts that Orr became a ward of the university without any vestige of free will. In fact, the court commented that Orr was clearly capable of taking care of himself—he was, after all, 22 years old and married with a child. The court reasoned that an athlete's participation in the program was voluntary, which certainly did not render him "less of an autonomous adult" or the institution "more of a caretaker."

With his claim against BYU soundly rejected by the court, Orr would now be forced to search elsewhere—his newly adopted homeland of Finland perhaps?—for financial compensation for his nagging pain in the back.

Tailgate Time 1

"Kickoff" Gumbo

Ingredients
3 large chicken breast halves (boneless, skinless)
salt
pepper
1 pound smoked sausage, thinly sliced
¼ cup vegetable oil
½ cup flour
5 tablespoons margarine
1 large onion, chopped
8 cloves garlic, minced
3 stalks celery, chopped
¼ cup Worcestershire sauce
4 cups hot water
5 beef bouillon cubes
1 14-ounce can of stewed tomatoes
2 cups frozen sliced okra
½ pound small shrimp, peeled

Cooking Instructions
- Season the chicken with salt and pepper. Heat the vegetable oil in a heavy cookware over medium-high heat. Cook the chicken until browned on both sides and remove. Add sausage and cook until browned, then remove.

Tailgate Time 1 (continued)

- To make the roux, sprinkle the flour over the vegetable oil, add 2 tablespoons of margarine and cook over medium heat, stirring constantly, until brown (about 10 minutes).
- Return to low heat and melt remaining 3 tablespoons margarine. Add onion, garlic, and celery. Cook for about 10 minutes.
- Add Worcestershire sauce, and salt and pepper to taste. Cook, while stirring frequently, for about 10 minutes.
- Add 4 cups hot water and bouillon cubes, whisking constantly. Add chicken, sausage, and shrimp.
- Bring to a boil, then reduce the heat, cover, and simmer for about 45 minutes. Add tomatoes and okra. Cover and simmer for about an hour.

Serves 6

Chapter Two

Female Field Goal Kicker: A Matter of Discrimination

Mercer v. Duke University, 181 F.Supp.2d 525 (M.D.N.C. 2001)

In this gender discrimination suit, Heather Mercer hotly contended that Duke University discriminated against her on the basis of her sex and therefore violated Title IX of the Education Amendments of 1972.

Mercer had been a successful field goal kicker for her high school team, and when she arrived at Duke, she went to the coach to discuss being considered as a walk-on for the all-male team. Although it was clear that Duke was not required by Title IX to afford females the opportunity to play football, the head coach, Fred Goldsmith, decided to give Mercer an audition on the spot.

Goldsmith, dressed in suit and tie, and Fred Chatham, the kicking coach, escorted her onto the field. Both Goldsmith and Chatham agreed that the conditions were not ideal because they were unable to snap the ball or hold it properly, and by her own admission, Mercer did not perform well that afternoon. After the tryout, Goldsmith informed Mercer that her skills were not quite where they needed to be, but that she could help the team in a managerial capacity instead.

Mercer thereafter attended all practices and games, assisted in winter conditioning, helped shag balls, and kept statistics for the team's place kickers. That spring, she participated in practice with the other players, including the intra-squad "Blue-White" scrimmage. Mercer's team trailed by one point and was in field goal range with one minute remaining. Goldsmith brought Mercer onto the field, where she successfully kicked a 28-yard field goal to win the game. An elated Goldsmith immediately announced that she had made the team.

Extensive publicity immediately followed the appointment of the first female on the Duke football team, and Goldsmith became concerned that the news might actually have an adverse effect on his players and on recruiting. Several newspaper articles made light of the situation, and Goldsmith began to discourage Mercer's participation. He told her, for example, that she would not be permitted to attend preseason camp. Mercer persisted, and Goldsmith suggested that perhaps she should consider other extracurricular activities like (and I kid you not) *beauty pageants.*

Arriving back at Duke that fall, Mercer met with Goldsmith, who told her that his decision to put her on the team was the worst decision he had ever made. Goldsmith was no doubt trying to be helpful (again, I kid you not) when he recommended that she consider trying out for the *cheerleading squad.* He commented on how pretty she was and compared her appearance to that of actress Molly Ringwald. As a final insult, Goldsmith then informed Mercer that she would not be allowed to suit up for games or to stand on the sidelines with the rest of the team.

The next year, Goldsmith called Mercer into his office and informed her that, alas, there was no place for her on the team. But here was the real problem: no member of the team, walk-on or otherwise, had *ever* been dismissed for performance reasons. It was also revealed that Goldsmith rarely observed Mercer's kicking. Mercer presented evidence of her superior kicking abilities that was in complete contrast to Goldsmith's alleged reasons for her dismissal.

Mercer had no other choice—she filed suit against Duke, claiming, among other things, gender discrimination. Based on the evidence presented, the jury found that Goldsmith had in fact discriminated against Mercer and that Duke was liable under Title IX. The jury awarded Mercer $1 in compensatory damages and an astounding $2 million in punitive damages.

In its posttrial motions, Duke contended that it was entitled to summary judgment because (1) the university had legitimate grounds for its conduct because Mercer lacked the qualifications to remain on the team, and (2) the president and athletic director were not on notice- of the allegations, as Mercer had not "formally" complained to any official at the university, and (3) Mercer failed to present sufficient evidence of deliberate indifference by the university.

Reasons for Duke's Actions

The court found that the jury could have reasonably concluded that Duke would not have made the same decisions with regard to Mercer had it not considered her gender. Mercer was the first person that Goldsmith had ever removed for "lack of ability." By Goldsmith's own admission, other place kickers on the team lacked the necessary skills to play in a game, yet they were not dismissed. And Mercer was the only player ever precluded from standing with the rest of the team on the sidelines.

Duke's Title IX Liability

The court held that in order for institutional liability to arise, the university official must simply have *knowledge* of the alleged discrimination. The source of that information was immaterial in determining whether liability attached. Both the president and the athletic director admitted that they were aware of Mercer's claim.

Because the president conceded that he first became aware of Mercer's claim of gender discrimination more than a year earlier, the court found sufficient evidence from which the jury could have reasonably determined that university officials responded with deliberate indifference to Mercer's federally protected right to be free from gender discrimination.

Punitive Damages

Duke also contended it was entitled to a new trial because the jury's punitive damages award was unconstitutionally excessive. In assessing that argument, the court considered (1) the degree of reprehensibility of the conduct, (2) whether the amount of the exemplary award bore a reasonable relationship to the compensatory award, and (3) the difference between the award and the civil or criminal penalties imposed in like cases.

In this regard, the court took note of the following:

- For more than two years, Goldsmith made adverse gender-based decisions concerning Mercer's membership on the team.
- Although officials were aware of Mercer's allegation of discrimination for much of that two-year period, the university took *no* action to correct Goldsmith's conduct toward her.

- Goldsmith's actions in (1) denying Mercer a uniform and pads, (2) issuing a press statement that Mercer would not be a part of the team, (3) requiring Mercer to leave the winter conditioning session, (4) making gender-based remarks to Mercer, and (5) precluding Mercer from even standing on the sidelines with the rest of the team were behavior that the jury could have found reprehensible enough to justify a substantial punitive damages award.

The court went further to suggest that modest awards of compensatory damages may properly support a higher ratio in punitive damages if (a) a particularly egregious act results in only limited economic damages, and (b) the monetary value of noneconomic harm is difficult to determine.

In this case, Mercer did not seek psychological counseling, which made the severity of her injury and the corresponding economic harm difficult to assess. However, Mercer did present evidence that Duke's conduct affected her mental and psychological health—she was constantly depressed, she was unable to function normally on a daily basis, she became extremely withdrawn, and her personality changed dramatically.

To the extent the jury found that Duke violated Title IX, the jury was also allowed to take the financial status of the defendant into account to ensure that the damages award had a deterrent effect. The court held that the $2 million in punitive damages had to be viewed in light of the purposes of such damages, and that a more modest sanction would likely have failed to achieve the desired result—of deterring discriminatory conduct of the sort that Duke committed against Mercer.

In the end, it turned out that Goldsmith's early words were prescient—that *was* the worst decision he ever made.

Tailgate Time 2

"Personal Foul" Chili

Ingredients

2 teaspoons cooking oil

2 onions, chopped

3 cloves garlic, minced

1 pound lean ground beef

¾ pound beef sirloin, cubed

1 15-ounce can of diced tomatoes

2 6-ounce cans of tomato paste

1 can of beef broth

3½ tablespoons chili sauce

1 tablespoon cumin

1 teaspoon oregano

1 teaspoon cayenne pepper

1 teaspoon salt

4 15-ounce cans of kidney beans

3 chili peppers, chopped

Cooking Instructions

- Heat cooking oil, and cook onions, garlic, and meat until brown.
- Add tomatoes, tomato paste, and beef broth.
- Add spices (chili sauce, cumin, oregano, cayenne pepper, salt).
- Stir in kidney beans and chili peppers.
- Reduce heat and simmer for 2 hours.

Serves 6

Chapter Three

The Chance to Play: Interpreting the Rehabilitation Act

Pahulu v. University of Kansas, 897 F.Supp. 1387 (D. Kan. 1995)

During a robust scrimmage, Alani Pahulu—who was on football scholarship at the University of Kansas—suffered a head injury after a hard tackle. He was briefly dazed and then began to feel numbness and tingling in his arms and legs. He managed to leave the field on his own, but he was not allowed to return.

A team physician subsequently examined Pahulu and diagnosed his episode as "transient quadriplegia." Another series of tests revealed that Pahulu had a congenitally narrow cervical canal. In consultation with a neurosurgeon at the KU Medical Center, the team physician concluded that Pahulu was at high risk for a potentially permanent neurological injury. Accordingly, the team physician disqualified Pahulu from any further participation on the squad.

Because Pahulu felt fine, he and his parents sought second opinions on the severity of his medical condition. The Pahulus saw three specialists, and their consensus was that Pahulu could participate in the sport with no more risk of permanent paralysis than any other player. Anxious to see their son play, the

Pahulus provided this information to the team physician, and they even offered to release and indemnify the university from liability should he be injured. The team physician and consulting neurosurgeon—although acknowledging their decision was conservative—remained firm in their refusal to let him play.

The Pahulus were not about to give up. Alleging a violation of the Rehabilitation Act of 1973, Pahulu filed suit against the university, seeking a preliminary injunction that would give him the chance to earn the *right* to a playing position (he was not asking the court to order the university play him). Pahulu explained that he was entering his last year of eligibility and that it was unlikely he could obtain a waiver from the NCAA for an additional year. If injunctive relief was not granted, his irreparable harm would include (1) the loss of a year of eligibility, and (2) the lessened opportunity for a professional sports career.

In order to succeed on the merits under the Rehabilitation Act, Pahulu had to establish a prima facie claim that (1) he was "disabled" within the meaning of the statute, and (2) he was "otherwise qualified" to participate in the program. The act provides that a recipient of federal financial assistance (like the university) may not discriminate on the basis of handicap, regardless of whether there is a rational basis for doing so. Therefore, the critical inquiry was whether the university had discriminated on the basis of the disability.

The Rehabilitation Act defines an "individual with a disability" as any person who has a "physical or mental impairment which substantially limits one or more of such person's major life activities." The statute requires two elements: first, that one has a physical or mental impairment, and second, that the impairment substantially limits one or more "major life activities." In the eyes of the court, Pahulu's status as disabled was fact-sensitive, requiring an individualized inquiry and a case-by-case determination.

The Chance to Play: Interpreting the Rehabilitation Act

On the disability issue, there was no question that the university regarded Pahulu's congenitally narrow cervical canal as a physical impairment. The university, however, contended that playing intercollegiate football was *not* a "major life activity" such as walking, seeing, hearing, speaking, breathing, learning, and working.

Pahulu contended that whether intercollegiate football participation was a major life activity was not an objective—but a *subjective*—determination. In other words, the question was whether playing college football was a major life activity for Pahulu, *not* for the general public. Pahulu testified that playing football provided him with a number of advantages: becoming a team player; learning discipline; being inspired to seek a better life; and watching his grades improve.

After hearing the testimony, the court concluded that intercollegiate football might have been a major life activity in Pahulu's education, but that the university's action was not a substantial limitation on Pahulu's opportunity to learn. The court observed that Pahulu's athletic scholarship continued on, allowing him access to the same academic resources that were previously available. Pahulu also had the opportunity to participate in the football program in a role other than as a player. The court also found persuasive the fact that the medical conclusion of the KU physicians was a reasonable one, and that it was supported by substantial and competent evidence for which the court was not willing to substitute its own opinion. Consequently, the court ruled that Pahulu was not disabled within the meaning of the Rehabilitation Act.

As a result, Pahulu did not suit up for the team that fall. He would never know for sure whether his spine could have taken the punishment of another year of college ball.

Tailgate Time 3

"Score Big" Salsa

Ingredients

1 28-ounce can of whole tomatoes

1 7-ounce can of green chiles, chopped

2 green onions (scallions), chopped

1 clove of garlic

1 tablespoon olive oil

2 teaspoons red wine vinegar

¼ teaspoon dried oregano

¼ cup chopped cilantro

salt

black pepper

Mixing Instructions

- Place tomatoes in mixing bowl and cut into small pieces.
- Mix together green chiles, green onions, garlic, olive oil, vinegar, and oregano. Add cilantro, salt, and pepper to taste.
- Refrigerate.

Yields 2 to 3 cups

Chapter Four

Paid Employee? A Player's Right to Workers' Compensation

Rensing v. Indiana State University, 437 N.E.2d 78 (Ind. App. 1982)

Fred Rensing was playing football at Indiana State University when he became permanently disabled from a spinal injury that occurred during the team's spring practice. Considering his injury just another workplace accident, Rensing applied to the Industrial Board for workers' compensation. His claim was denied on the ground that an employer-employee relationship did not exist between him and the school's board of trustees.

Rensing filed for judicial review of the hearing, asserting that as a scholarship athlete, he was an employee of the university. Trial testimony revealed that the trustees, through their agent (the head football coach), offered Rensing a scholarship. Under the financial aid agreement—which was renewable annually for four years, provided that Rensing actively participated on the team—Rensing received free tuition, room, board, laboratory fees, book allowance, tutoring, and a limited number of football tickets for family and friends. This agreement provided that the financial aid would continue even if Rensing suffered an injury that would make it inadvisable for him to play.

In defending the claim, the university trustees conceded that some manner of contract existed between them and Rensing. However, they argued—and the Industrial Board agreed—that there was no contract for employment within the meaning of the workers' compensation act. Rensing contended that his agreement to play football (or, if he was injured, to otherwise assist the football program) in return for financial assistance *was* a contract for employment.

The court—surprisingly enough—agreed with Rensing. The court reasoned that the workers' compensation statute was to be interpreted liberally. Consequently, in applying the statutory definition of "employee," a measure of generosity was warranted so that an injured worker, or his dependents, would not be deprived of benefits.

The court initially focused on the definitions of "employer" and "employee" in the act. Since college sports participants were not *expressly* excluded, the court decided that the central question was whether there was a "written or implied" contract that obligated Rensing to play football in return for the scholarship he received.

The court found inescapable the conclusion that the trustees had in fact contracted with Rensing to play football at the university. The parties' agreement clearly anticipated not only that Rensing would play football in return for his scholarship, but that in the event he suffered an injury, he would assist in other tasks. Rensing's academic benefits would continue as long as he was "otherwise eligible to compete." In light of such language, the court dismissed the trustees' suggestion that Rensing's benefits were only a "grant" to further his education.

Additionally, the court noted that trustees retained their right to terminate Rensing's award if he: (1) failed to satisfy the university's and the NCAA's academic requirements for scholarships, (2) voluntarily rendered himself ineligible for intercollegiate competition, (3) fraudulently misrepresented any information on his application, letter of intent, or tender, or (4) engaged in serious misconduct warranting substantial disciplinary penalty by the university. This right of termination tended to distinguish Rensing's grant from an outright gift, and it was a significant factor indicating an employer-employee relationship. The court concluded that Rensing and the trustees bargained for an exchange of Rensing's football talents for certain scholarship benefits—much like an employer and employee would.

Having decided that Rensing was an "employee," the court then had to determine whether his employment was "casual" so as to bring it outside the statute's coverage. The court concluded that Rensing's employment was *not* casual, since it clearly was "periodically regular," even though not permanent. The evidence revealed that football was a daily routine for 16 weeks each year, and that during the off-season the student-athlete had to work out on a daily basis to maintain his skills.

The workers' compensation act required that the employment be in the "course of the trade or business of such employer," and the court recognized that maintaining a football team is an important aspect of the university's educational mission, even if such athletic endeavors were not the university's principal occupation. It was uncontroverted that the university's nationally recognized football program had increased enrollment. As a result, the court held that Rensing was entitled to workers' compensation benefits.

A vigorous dissent followed. It agreed that a measure of liberality should be applied in defining who is an employee, and it conceded that student-athletes have entered into a contract of sorts. But the minority opinion was fairly confident that the state legislature never intended for athletes to be considered "employees" within the meaning of workers' compensation.

Tailgate Time 4

"Time Out" Hot Cheese Dip

Ingredients

2 cups mild cheddar cheese, shredded

8 ounces cream cheese

1½ cups sour cream

¼ cup mild green chile peppers, chopped

jalapeno peppers, finely chopped

⅓ cup green onions, chopped

⅛ teaspoon Worcestershire sauce

Cooking Instructions

- In a medium bowl, mix well cheddar and cream cheese, sour cream, chile peppers, green onions, and Worcester sauce.
- Bake at 350° F. for 1 hour.

Yields about 4 cups

Chapter Five

A Matter of Image: The Parameters of Publicity

Kimbrough v. Coca-Cola/USA, 521 S.W.2d 719 (Tex. Civ. App.—Eastland 1975)

One man's publicity, it appears, is another man's poison.

John Kimbrough sued Coca-Cola and related sports publishers, seeking damages for the unauthorized exploitation of his name, image, and reputation in a well-publicized advertising program. The defendants published a series of commercials in local sports publications, and the issue was whether they had adequately secured Kimbrough's permission to use his name and photograph in this regard.

Under the defendants' plan, the sports information directors of each of the various Southwest Conference schools were contacted to nominate a former football player as the school's outstanding player. The selected player was then notified that he would appear in a painting honoring the top players in the conference. Each player would receive an original painting, with reproductions to be sent to his university and to the Texas Sports Hall of Fame. The notification also suggested that the paintings might be used in "institutional advertisements." Kimbrough was selected to represent Texas A&M, and according to the defendants, he clearly accepted.

Kimbrough, on the other hand, denied that he had ever contemplated the use of his name and picture in an advertisement that had the commercial aspects of the one published, and that he had never consented to such use. Kimbrough brought suit, pleading multiple theories of recovery: violation of an absolute proprietary right, invasion of the right of privacy, fraud and misrepresentation, quantum meruit, and unjust enrichment.

Defendants contended that the facts clearly indicated that Kimbrough was a public figure, and because the advertisement was not offensive or derogatory, its publication would not be actionable even if Kimbrough had not consented. This situation presented a novel issue for the court—whether a public figure had a right of privacy against the unauthorized use of his name and photograph for commercial purposes.

The court recognized that although no such cause of action existed under the common law in Texas, several jurisdictions had acknowledged such a right. The Supreme Courts of Alabama and New Jersey, for example, ruled that while a public character necessarily relinquishes a part of his right of privacy, such waiver is limited to that which is necessary and proper for public information. In other words, the privacy of a public figure may not be appropriated through the use of his name and photograph for commercial purposes unless it is essential to legitimate news value. To exploit one's name, reputation, or accomplishments would be grossly unfair, according to the ruling.

The court could find no Texas case directly in point, but it did note that the right of privacy was generally recognized under such theories as libel and slander. The court conceded that Kimbrough had legitimately pleaded a cause of action for the unauthorized exploitation of his name and likeness, and that such a suit was justiciable in Texas.

The defendants then argued that the use of Kimbrough's name and likeness was actually made with his consent. In support of its contention, the defendants presented the following letter from Sports Communications, Inc., to Kimbrough:

Dear John:

Recently Dave Campbell's TEXAS FOOTBALL Magazine and Coca-Cola have planned a series of paintings that will honor the top players in Southwest Conference football history. You have been selected by Texas A&M University as the outstanding football player in its history, and we look forward with enthusiasm to your approval of the project.

I enclose a copy of one of the series of paintings, which we have commissioned. Coca-Cola and TEXAS FOOTBALL Magazine will present to you the original painting, and, in addition, framed reproductions of the painting will be given to Texas A&M University. Another reproduction is being presented to the new Texas Sports Hall of Fame. There is also a contemplated use of these paintings in a series of institutional advertisements in behalf of college football, in Dave Campbell's TEXAS FOOTBALL Magazines.

While no endorsement of any product is implied in the institutional nature of the proposed usage, we would not, of course, approach a project of this type without your complete approval. We would appreciate hearing from you as early as it is convenient to do so.

Sincerely,

Bill Sansing

Kimbrough responded to the letter as follows (clearly indicating his consent to the project, according to the defendants):

Dear Mr. Sansing,
I have received your letter concerning Texas Football Magazine and Coca-Cola paintings and I am honored to represent Texas A&M.
I am looking forward to meeting.
Sincerely,
John Kimbrough

When asked about this correspondence in his deposition, Kimbrough testified this way:

Q: Did you answer yes to Mr. Sansing's letter?
A: I agreed to pose for the picture or whatever you call it, you know.
Q: Is that what you mean when you answered yes?
A: Yes. That was our interpretation of it.

The court explained that in order for consent to be asserted as a defense, the consent must be as broad as the act complained of. Consent that has been exceeded is *not* a valid defense.

With the matter up in the air, the court ruled that a nagging question of fact still existed as to the *extent* of the consent given by Kimbrough. The case was therefore remanded for a determination of whether his letter was sufficient to waive his privacy claims. There the trial court could ponder—and eventually determine—the exact meaning of the word *yes*.

Tailgate Time 5

"The Wave" Shrimp on a Stick

Ingredients

24 extra large shrimp (about 1½ pounds), peeled

24 fresh basil leaves

24 thin strips bacon

24 bamboo skewers (8 to 10 inches long)

Cooking Instructions

- Insert bamboo skewer running the length of the shrimp. Place a basil leaf on the back of the shrimp, and wrap the shrimp in bacon.
- Set grill to high temperature.
- Arrange the shrimp on grate and cook until the bacon is browned and the shrimp are cooked, turning the kebabs every minute or so to ensure even cooking.

Serves 6

PART II

COACHES

Chapter Six

Alcoholism as a Disability: Distinguishing On-the-Job Conduct

Maddox v. University of Tennessee, 907 F.Supp. 1144 (E.D. Tenn. 1994)

Robert Maddox was an assistant football coach at the University of Tennessee, and shortly after he assumed his coaching duties, he was arrested by the Knoxville police, who charged him with drunk driving. Maddox was eventually fired for the infraction.

According to newspaper reports, Maddox backed his automobile across a public road at a high rate of speed and almost struck another vehicle. When stopped, Maddox was combative and refused to take a breathalyzer test. Maddox then lied to the officer, stating that he was unemployed. The arresting officer noted on the warrant that Maddox's clothing was disorderly and his pants unzipped.

On the day after his arrest, Maddox met with the head coach, and he was told that as long as he completed a rehabilitation program, he could keep his job. He soon entered a hospital to begin a course of treatment. About two weeks later, he received a call from the head coach, who informed him that he was being placed on administrative leave. Shortly thereafter, Maddox received a letter of termination.

Taking the only route seemingly available to him—that of an indignant victim—Maddox sued the university, its board of trustees, and its athletic director for relief under the Americans with Disabilities Act and the Rehabilitation Act of 1973, alleging that he was wrongfully discharged because he suffered from the debilitating disability of alcoholism.

The testimony subsequently revealed that Maddox completed a lengthy application for the assistant coach's position. The following are a few poignant examples of his answers:

- To the question "Describe any health problems or physical limitations which would limit your ability to perform the duties of the position for which you are applying," Maddox replied "None."
- To the question "Have you ever been arrested for a criminal offense of any kind?," Maddox replied "No."

It appeared at trial that Maddox had taken some "liberties" with the truth. It transpired that Maddox had suffered from alcoholism *before* he came to the University of Tennessee, and that he had received treatment for this condition while working in a previous job. He insisted that his response to the question about "health problems or physical limitations" was completely accurate because, "It never affected my coaching ability. I never drank on the job." And regarding his criminal history, it was revealed that Maddox had been arrested three times before he was hired by the university—once for possession of a controlled substance and twice for driving under the influence of alcohol. Not surprisingly, Maddox never attempted to explain that discrepancy.

According to Maddox, no one at the university told him why he was fired, except that a trainer confided that "the athletic director and a couple of people from the board of trustees and athletic association wanted to get rid of [Maddox] as fast as possible so they wouldn't have to deal with having another alcoholic in the program." Maddox named two other coaches who had been convicted of drunken driving, but who had managed to keep their positions. Maddox also denied that as an assistant coach he had any responsibility for serving as a role model to athletes, or for counseling them.

The defendant's position concerning the termination of Maddox's employment was reflected in the athletic director's affidavit:

> My decision to terminate Maddox's employment was based solely on the actions which he had engaged in during the course of his DUI arrest and his prior undisclosed DUI arrests, and my judgment that Maddox could no longer effectively carry out the responsibilities of an assistant football coach at The University of Tennessee.
>
> Neither alcoholism nor any treatment Maddox may have received for that alcoholism played any role whatever in my decision to terminate Maddox's employment.

The athletic director added that had he known of the Maddox's prior convictions, he would not have hired him.

There was no evidence that before his arrest Maddox discussed his alcoholism with any of his superiors, or sought rehabilitative treatment. Maddox submitted the affidavit of a former colleague at the University of Louisville to establish that Maddox's treatment for alcoholism did not interfere with his performance of his coaching duties.

In evaluating the case, the court first looked at the Rehabili-tation Act of 1973, which provided that "no otherwise qualified individual with a disability shall, solely by reason of her or his disability, be excluded from the participation in, be denied the benefits of, or be subjected to discrimination under any program or activity receiving federal financial assistance." The elements of Maddox's cause of action under the Rehabilitation Act were as follows: (1) Maddox was a "handicapped person" under the act, (2) he was "otherwise qualified" for participation in the program, and (3) he was being excluded from participation in the program solely because of his handicap.

The court conceded that the issues of (a) whether a plaintiff was an otherwise qualified disabled individual, and (b) whether a defendant employer was able to reasonably accommodate its disabled employee were intertwined. Whether an individual was "otherwise qualified" depended upon whether he could meet the necessary requirements of the position, and what constituted the necessary requirements of a position depended on the extent to which an employer could satisfy the legitimate interests of both itself and the disabled employee.

While Maddox bore the burden of proving these elements, the court did not require him to establish that the defendant's discrimi-nation was intentional. A prima facie case under the Rehabilitation Act required proof of termination solely on the basis of the disabil-ity. If the defendant could show a nondiscriminatory reason for its action, then the plaintiff had to prove that the reasons advanced by the defendant were merely pretextual.

The court noted the critical distinction between a disability—which *cannot* be the basis of an adverse employment action—and conduct on the part of an otherwise qualified individual with a disability—which *can* justify the same action taken against an employee with no disability.

Maddox relied heavily on a previous judicial decision that reasoned that since drunk driving was a manifestation of the handicap of alcoholism, the employer's actions were assumed to be based upon the employee's alcoholism, and the burden was on the *employer* to show that the employee was not otherwise qualified. Maddox pointed out that there was no evidence that his alcoholism had caused him to be tardy or absent, that he had been intoxicated on the job, or that alcoholism had interfered with his work performance.

The court, however, found this argument unpersuasive, noting that if Maddox's argument were accepted, an employer would be required to accommodate *all* behavior of an alcoholic that was related to the use of intoxicating beverages. The court refused to hold that an action taken in response to conduct caused by a disability is the same as an action taken on the basis of the disability itself.

While alcoholism might compel one to drink intoxicating beverages, there was no evidence that it compelled Maddox to operate a motor vehicle or engage in the other conduct described by the police. The court found it unnecessary to consider the issue of reasonable accommodation, because the decision to terminate Maddox's employment was made on the basis of specific conduct—*not* on the basis of Maddox's disability—and therefore his termination did not violate the Rehabilitation Act.

In granting the university's summary judgment motion, the court was mindful of the Supreme Court's requirement that an employer needs to conduct an individualized inquiry and determine whether a disabled person was otherwise qualified for a position. In this case—in spite of the evidence submitted by Maddox that might raise issues of fact—the record clearly established that the university discharged Maddox not because of his alcoholism, but because of criminal conduct that the university deemed embarrassing.

Regardless of whether it might have been more compassionate to retain Maddox and assist him in his struggle with alcoholism, the Rehabilitation Act does not require such a course of action, and to discuss the extent to which an athletic department can accommodate an alcoholic coach would be to stray into the forbidden territory of an advisory opinion.

As to Maddox's cause of action under the Americans with Disabilities Act, the court noted that references in the ADA to the Rehabilitation Act argued in favor of consistent constructions of the two acts. The ADA (unlike the Rehabilitation Act) expressly provides that an employee who is an alcoholic can be held to the same standards of other employees—even if unsatisfactory behavior is related to the alcoholism. Congress thus explicitly recognizes the distinction between a disability and conduct related to a disability.

The court reasoned that if the university could have discharged a nonalcoholic employee for similar conduct, then the provisions of the ADA would sustain Maddox's termination. Because Maddox failed to prove discrimination due to his disability—rather than his decidedly unruly conduct—the university was, at long last, entitled to summary judgment.

Tailgate Time 6

"Back to the Gridiron" Grilled Corn on the Cob

Ingredients

6 medium ears of sweet corn

½ cup butter

2 tablespoons fresh basil, minced

2 tablespoons fresh parsley, minced

½ teaspoon salt

Cooking Instructions

- Soak corn in cold water for 20 minutes.
- In a small bowl, combine butter, basil, parsley, and salt.
- Carefully peel back corn husks, and spread butter mixture over corn.
- Rewrap corn in husks and secure with string. Grill corn, covered, over medium heat for about 30 minutes or until tender, turning occasionally.

Serves 6

Chapter Seven

Employment Contract: The Liquidated Damages Clause

Vanderbilt University v. DiNardo, 174 F.3d 751 (6th Cir. 1999)

Coaching can be a fickle world, and enticements to leave for greener pastures are, it seems, always an issue.

Gerry DiNardo resigned as head football coach at Vanderbilt to take the same position at Louisiana State. Apparently not amused, Vanderbilt brought a breach of contract action under the parties' employment agreement, and the university sought a substantial reimbursement under the liquidated damages clause.

Section one of the employment contract provided for a five-year term and, most significantly, it expressed the university's desire for stability:

> The University hereby agrees to hire Mr. DiNardo for a period of five (5) years from the date hereof with Mr. DiNardo's assurance that he will serve the entire term of this Contract, a long-term commitment by Mr. DiNardo being important to the University's desire for a stable intercollegiate football program.

The reciprocal liquidated damages provision provided that should DiNardo be replaced as coach, Vanderbilt would pay him his remaining salary. And should DiNardo leave before his contract expired, DiNardo would reimburse the university for the remainder of his contract. Section eight of the contract began:

> Mr. DiNardo recognizes that his promise to work for the University for the entire term of this 5-year Contract is of the essence of this Contract to the University. Mr. DiNardo also recognizes that the University is making a highly valuable investment in his continued employment by entering into this Contract and its investment would be lost were he to resign or otherwise terminate his employment as Head Football Coach with the University prior to the expiration of this Contract.

Then the provision stated:

> Accordingly, Mr. DiNardo agrees that in the event he resigns or otherwise terminates his employment as Head Football Coach (as opposed to his resignation or termination from another position at the University to which he may have been reassigned), prior to the expiration of this Contract, and is employed or performing services for a person or institution other than the University, he will pay to the University as liquidated damages an amount equal to his Base Salary, less amounts that would otherwise be deducted or withheld from his Base Salary for income and social security tax purposes, multiplied by the number of years (or portion(s) thereof) remaining on the Contract.

With a little over a year remaining on the contract, DiNardo and Paul Hoolahan, Vanderbilt's athletic director, discussed a two-year extension. DiNardo signed the addendum, but told Hoolahan that he wanted to discuss it with his brother Larry DiNardo, a lawyer.

Shortly thereafter, LSU contacted Vanderbilt in hopes of speaking with DiNardo about becoming its head coach. Hoolahan gave DiNardo permission to do so, and a few weeks later, DiNardo announced he was accepting the position at LSU.

As might be expected, Vanderbilt sent a demand letter to DiNardo, asking for payment of liquidated damages under the contract. Vanderbilt believed that DiNardo was liable for three years of his net salary: one year under the original contract and two years under the addendum. DiNardo did not respond to Vanderbilt's demand.

Vanderbilt accordingly brought suit against DiNardo, and both parties filed motions for summary judgment. The district court held that section eight was an enforceable liquidated damages provision—*not* an unlawful penalty—and that the damages were reasonable. The court also held that the addendum was enforceable and that Vanderbilt did not waive its contractual rights when it granted DiNardo permission to talk to LSU. The court accordingly entered judgment against DiNardo for $281,886.

DiNardo appealed, arguing that the district court erred in concluding: (1) that the liquidated damages provision was not an unlawful penalty, (2) that Vanderbilt did not waive its right to liquidated damages, (3) that the addendum to the contract was enforceable, and (4) that the addendum applied to the damages provision of the original contract.

Liquidated Damages or Unenforceable Penalty

DiNardo first claimed that section eight of the contract was not a liquidated damages provision but a "thinly disguised, overly broad non-compete provision" that was unenforceable under Tennessee law.

In Tennessee, a liquidated damages provision is considered valid if it is (1) reasonable in relation to the anticipated damages occurring from the breach, and (2) not grossly disproportionate to the actual damages. When these conditions are met, particularly the first, the provision is deemed an enforceable clause. However, if there is any doubt, the provision will generally be found to be a penalty.

DiNardo, however, contended that there was no evidence that the parties contemplated that the potential damage from his resignation would go beyond the cost of hiring a replacement coach. He argued that his salary bore no relationship to Vanderbilt's damages and that the liquidated damages amount was unreasonable.

The Sixth Circuit thought otherwise. In its view, the contractual language clearly established that Vanderbilt wanted a long-term commitment because it was important to a stable football program, and this commitment was "of the essence" to the contract. The court held that the use of a formula to calculate liquidated damages was reasonable given the nature of the unquantifiable damages in the case. Parties to a contract may include consequential damages as long as they are clearly contemplated. The potential damage to Vanderbilt extended beyond the cost of merely hiring a new coach, and it was this uncertain potential—estimating how the loss of a head football coach would affect alumni relations, public support, football ticket sales, contributions, and so on—that the parties sought to address by providing for a sum certain.

The court rejected DiNardo's argument that a question of fact remained as to whether the parties intended section eight to be a "reasonable estimate" of damages. The liquidated damages were in line with Vanderbilt's estimate of its actual damages: $27,000 for expenses of recruiting a new head coach; $86,840 for moving expenses of the new coaching staff; and $184,311 for the compensation difference between the coaching staffs. In the court's view, these stipulated damages clauses were eminently reasonable.

Waiver

DiNardo next argued that Vanderbilt waived its right to liquidated damages when it granted DiNardo permission to discuss the coaching position with LSU. Under Tennessee law, a party may not recover liquidated damages if it is responsible for nonperformance of the contract.

The court held that Vanderbilt did not waive its rights by giving DiNardo permission to pursue the LSU position. First of all, Hoolahan's permission for DiNardo to interview with LSU was circumscribed—Hoolahan gave DiNardo permission only to talk to LSU about the position; he did not authorize DiNardo to terminate his contract with Vanderbilt. Secondly, the employment contract required DiNardo to ask Vanderbilt's athletic director for permission to speak with another school, and granting such permission was a "professional courtesy." The parties anticipated that DiNardo could explore other coaching positions, subject to the terms of the liquidated damages provision.

Addendum

DiNardo argued that the original employment contract explicitly provided that section eight was limited to "the entire term of this five-year contract," and that the addendum did not extend the effective date of section eight, unlike other sections in the contract. The court disagreed, holding that the plain and unambiguous language provided for the wholesale extension of the *entire* contract.

DiNardo also claimed that the addendum never became a binding contract because his brother Larry DiNardo never expressly approved its terms. Under Tennessee law, parties can accept terms of a contract and make it conditional upon some other event. DiNardo argued that the addendum was not enforceable because it was contingent on Larry DiNardo's approval.

Vanderbilt responded that that there was no condition precedent to the addendum's enforceability. If Larry DiNardo found the language objectionable, he should have said so immediately, and if his approval was a condition precedent, it was satisfied by his failure to object. There was evidence that Coach DiNardo told others he was happy with the extension, which strongly implied that it was finalized.

The majority opinion of the Sixth Circuit decided that ultimately there was a disputed question of material fact as to whether the addendum was enforceable. The dispute revolved around whether Larry DiNardo's approval of the contract was a condition precedent to the addendum's enforceability. The court said it simply could not resolve the issue on summary judgment—there was some evidence from which a jury could find that Larry DiNardo's failure to object did *not* amount to acceptance of the addendum.

Therefore, the appellate court affirmed the district court's judgment that the contract contained an enforceable liquidated damages provision. But the district court's holding that the

Employment Contract: The Liquidated Damages Clause

addendum was enforceable as a matter of law was reversed and remanded for resolution of whether Larry DiNardo's approval was a condition precedent, and if so, whether the condition was satisfied by Larry DiNardo's failure to object.

Not all of the justices agreed. One justice believed that granting a *full* summary judgment to Vanderbilt was appropriate because the evidence supported the conclusion that the contract was agreed upon, that Larry DiNardo failed to object to the contract extension, and that the coach himself confirmed the deal was done.

Another justice argued that section eight was designed to function as a *penalty*, not as a liquidation of the university's damages, because of the following:

- Damages to the university from DiNardo's premature resignation would be the same whether or not he took a job elsewhere, and liquidated damages were not imposed unless he accepted another job. How the coach spent his post-resignation time should not affect the university's damages. If the coach chose to lie on a beach, the university would suffer the same damages.
- Damages arising from the need to replace a departing coach should not vary according to the number of years left on the coach's contract.

In the end, one can only hope that Coach DiNardo—now poorer by the sum of $281,886 (not to mention his attorney's fees)—had counted on this considerable expense when he negotiated his contract with LSU.

Tailgate Time 7

"First Down" Baked Potato Wedges

Ingredients

6 large potatoes
¼ cup olive oil
1 tablespoon paprika
1 tablespoon garlic powder
1 tablespoon chili powder
1 tablespoon onion powder

Cooking Instructions

- Preheat oven to 450° F.
- Cut potatoes into wedges.
- Mix together olive oil, paprika, garlic powder, chili powder, and onion powder. Coat potatoes with this oil/spice mixture and place on baking sheet.
- Bake for 45 minutes in preheated oven.

Serves 6

Chapter Eight

Not for Attribution: The Claim for Defamation

McGarry v. University of San Diego, 154 Cal. App. 4th 97 (2007)

In a series of unfortunate events, the venerable Kevin McGarry was fired by the University of San Diego as its head football coach, prompting him to file a defamation lawsuit against the university and two of its officials, Mary Lyons (its president) and Robert Pastoor (its vice president of student affairs).

The defamation claims were premised, first of all, on statements contained in a unflattering newspaper article published in the *San Diego Union-Tribune* two days after McGarry's termination, and secondly, on somewhat vague statements made by Lyons during a meeting with the parents of the team members.

McGarry had been employed by the university for 26 years. He had been the head coach for the past seven years, and had been named coach of the year. Shortly before he was fired, the university hired JoAnn Nestor as the new athletic director. McGarry and Nestor had a terse exchange, prompting McGarry to lodge a complaint against her with the human resources department. In what appeared to be a retaliatory move, Nestor then approached McGarry and said there had been a complaint by trainers that he had kicked a football at them during practice. McGarry explained that footballs were routinely removed from the field as a safety precaution, but that he had never aimed at anyone.

Nestor later sent an interoffice memo that purported to confirm their discussion concerning the football-kicking incident and to memorialize McGarry's admission that he had kicked a football toward a player out of frustration. McGarry received a copy of Nestor's memo with written instructions to report to Vice President Pastoor's office the following day. When McGarry arrived, he was told his employment had been terminated.

Shortly thereafter, an article appeared in the local newspaper stating that "a series of 'incidents' over the past two months led to McGarry's termination, several sources at the school reported." The article recited that the coaches and staff had been informed of the termination and were explicitly told "not to comment publicly about it."

Although the article stated that Pastoor and Nestor declined to comment because of "confidentiality related to personnel matters," the article went on to explain that "several university officials, speaking on the condition of anonymity, outlined a 'culmination of events'" that led to the termination. The article later stated that "the sources said several incidents in particular led to McGarry's immediate termination."

Lyons and Pastoor then held a closed-door meeting with parents of the players to discuss the situation and to introduce the interim head coach. At that meeting, several parents asked whether there were other reasons. Lyons responded that she could not comment.

One parent asked, "Was it a criminal or moral issue? Yes or No? If you say yes, I'll back you 100 percent. If you say no, your timing's bad and I can't back you anymore." Lyons responded, "To our knowledge, Coach McGarry was not involved in any criminal activity."

McGarry's defamation claims were based on the newspaper article and on Lyons's statement at the meeting with parents. McGarry claimed that the university and Pastoor were responsible for leaking the accusations contained in the article, and that the incidents described were either false or were routine disagreements between coaches. He also claimed that Lyons's comments to the parents carried an implication that McGarry had committed immoral acts that warranted his dismissal.

Defamation

The court remarked that a threshold determination in any defamation action is whether the plaintiff is a public figure. A public figure must show not only that the statement was false but that it was made with knowledge that it was false or with reckless disregard for the truth.

It was clear that McGarry occupied a high-profile position in San Diego's athletic community, and the abrupt termination of his employment—coming in the middle of a successful season and on the eve of an important game—was an important issue to the public. In spite of this, McGarry contended that the more stringent malice standards did not apply because the position he held and the reasons for his termination did not affect the general public in any appreciable way.

The court disagreed. It noted that Lyons did not expressly assert that McGarry's employment had been terminated because of immoral behavior, and therefore it neither contained nor implied a provably false assertion of fact. At most, it was an opinion, which was not actionable. Furthermore, Lyons believed her statement to be true, and it was based on information received from supposedly reliable sources.

Anti-SLAPP Motion

The defendants also filed motions to strike the defamation claims under what was known as the anti-SLAPP (Strategic Lawsuit Against Public Participation) statute. This law provided that free speech lawsuits were subject to a special motion to strike unless the plaintiff could establish a high probability of prevailing on the claim. The statute was intended to encourage public debate by allowing a court to promptly dismiss clearly unmeritorious claims that were brought to chill the defendant's right to free speech.

The trial court granted the defendants' anti-SLAPP motion. On appeal, McGarry argued that the law was inapplicable because none of the statements qualified as protected speech. The appellate court, however, agreed with the trial court that the defendants' statements were protected speech and therefore subject to dismissal under the statute.

The Shield Law Motion

McGarry moved to compel the deposition of the newspaper's reporter to at least confirm that the statements contained in the article were made by university officials. The newspaper opposed the motion, asserting that the Shield Law protected a reporter's sources and created an absolute immunity against disclosure. The court agreed and denied McGarry's motion to compel the deposition.

In the end, a bitter Coach McGarry was forced to walk away from the courthouse with nothing but a flimsy newspaper clipping and his deeply held suspicions about who leaked the tawdry news of his termination to the press.

Tailgate Time 8

"Quarterback" Potato Salad

Ingredients
2 pounds potatoes (about 5 cups), peeled and diced
½ cup hard-boiled eggs, chopped
½ cup mayonnaise
2 tablespoons cider vinegar
1 cup celery, diced
½ cup onion, chopped
2 tablespoons parsley, chopped
1 teaspoon salt
¼ teaspoon black pepper

Cooking Instructions
- Boil potatoes in large pot for about 15 minutes until tender. Cut into small pieces.
- In large bowl combine egg, mayonnaise, vinegar, celery, onion, parsley, salt, and pepper.
- Mix thoroughly with potatoes and other ingredients.

Serves 6

Chapter Nine

Suing the University: The Uphill Battle of Sovereign Immunity

Johnson v. Sorensen, 914 So.2d 830 (Ala. 2005)

Due to no fault of his own, Ellis Johnson—an assistant football coach at the University of Alabama—was abruptly fired from his job. Johnson sued the university and its board of trustees for breach of their employment contract. The university moved to dismiss the complaint by asserting the defense of sovereign immunity.

By way of brief background, the university had recently hired Mike Dubose as its head football coach, and shortly thereafter, Johnson was offered a position as assistant coach. Johnson's employment contract provided that he could be terminated with or without cause. The contract also contained a liquidated damages clause providing that if Johnson were terminated without cause, the university would pay him the "amount of the current annual base salary due for the remainder of the term of the contract then in effect."

The contract then provided for judicial enforcement of the liquidated damages clause: "Failure to timely pay such liquidated damages shall constitute a breach of this contract, and such sum shall be recoverable, together with reasonable attorney's fees, in any such court of competent jurisdiction."

Perhaps even more important—as it eventually transpired—was the following anti-waiver provision of the contract: "It is expressly agreed and understood between the parties that nothing contained herein shall be construed to constitute a waiver by the university of its right to claim such exemptions, privileges, and immunities as may be provided by law."

Dubose was subsequently terminated as head coach, and because his employment was tied to that of Dubose, Johnson too was fired. Johnson was offered a lower paying job with The Citadel, and he asked the University of Alabama to give him—as a form of settlement—an amount equal to the difference between his current salary and that offered by The Citadel.

Johnson's proposal was rejected, so he sued the University of Alabama, its president, and its athletic director. Johnson contended that the president and athletic director had fraudulently suppressed the fact that the liquidated damages clause was not "enforceable" as specifically provided in his employment contract. Johnson said he would never have entered into an employment contract had he known there was no way to enforce it.

Following a hearing, the trial court granted the university's summary judgment motion. Johnson appealed only from the summary judgment entered on the fraud claims asserted against the president and athletic director—not those of the university.

In analyzing the suit, the Alabama Supreme Court first considered the state's constitution, which provided for governmental immunity. This immunity, the court held, extended to the state's institutions of higher learning, and to state officers and employees acting in their official capacities. Because the president and athletic director were engaged in negotiating Johnson's employment contract, they were entitled to state-agent immunity unless their conduct took them outside the scope of protection. Additionally, the constitution provided that those dealing with the state were charged with knowledge of this doctrine.

In order to establish a prima facie claim of fraudulent suppression, a plaintiff has to produce substantial evidence establishing that:

- the defendant had a duty to disclose an existing material fact,
- the defendant suppressed that fact,
- the defendant had actual knowledge of the fact,
- the defendant's suppression of the fact induced the plaintiff to act or to refrain from acting, and
- the plaintiff suffered actual damage as a proximate result.

The president testified that that he gave Johnson's contract only a cursory reading and that he never discussed employment contracts in any detail with the university's counsel. The president said he knew universities were immune from certain suits, but he did not know whether Johnson could legally enforce his employment contract.

The athletic director testified that he assumed the contract was binding and enforceable, but that he did not understand the meaning of the term "sovereign immunity." He said he did not convey any information to Johnson regarding sovereign immunity.

Johnson testified that no one at the university explained sovereign immunity to him, but that he was generally aware of the doctrine and that he had previously hired a sports lawyer.

The court found critical the provision in Johnson's contract that nothing could be construed as a *waiver* by the university of any privileges or immunities. After reviewing the record, the court concluded that Johnson failed to establish a prima facie case of fraudulent suppression. In the court's eyes, Johnson failed to show that the president or athletic director owed him a duty to disclose the applicability of the doctrine of sovereign immunity to his contract.

Furthermore, the court noted, those dealing with the state are charged with knowledge of its immunity. Nothing in the record indicated that the negotiations over Johnson's employment were anything other than an arm's length transaction.

Coach Johnson therefore learned the hard way that the battle to overcome sovereign immunity is a significant one—even for a grizzled coach used to a rigorous contact sport.

Tailgate Time 9

"Touchdown Time" Chicken Wings

Ingredients

12 chicken wings

⅔ cup flour

¼ teaspoon paprika

¼ teaspoon cayenne pepper

¼ teaspoon salt

cooking oil

⅓ cup butter

⅓ cup hot sauce

⅓ teaspoon garlic powder

⅓ teaspoon black pepper

Cooking Instructions

- Mix together in a small bowl the flour, paprika, cayenne pepper, and salt.
- Place chicken wings in bowl and sprinkle flour mixture on top until evenly coated. Refrigerate for about one hour.
- Heat oil in deep fryer, and fry the coated wings for about 15 minutes.
- Combine butter, hot sauce, garlic powder, and black pepper in small saucepan over low heat. Stir until mixture is well blended.

Tailgate Time 9 (continued)

- Place wings in serving bowl, add butter mixture, and stir together well.

Serves 6

Chapter Ten

Perk City: Enforcing the Coach's Contract

Rodgers v. Georgia Tech Athletic Ass'n, 303 S.E.2d 467 (Ga. 1983)

As these things happen, Franklin "Pepper" Rodgers was fired from his job as head coach at Georgia Tech. Rodgers was given the axe by the board of the athletic association, notwithstanding the fact that he had a written employment contract. In addition to salary, health insurance, and pension benefits, the contract provided that Rodgers was entitled to certain "perquisites"—or fringe benefits—as he became eligible for them.

In his breach of contract action, Rodgers made no claim for base salary, health insurance, and pension plan benefits, since all of those were voluntarily provided by the athletic association through the expiration date of the contract. His claim was solely for the value of various fringe benefits, and that is where the gist of the dispute lay.

Both parties moved for summary judgment, and the trial court granted the association's motion. Rodgers appealed, and he listed some two dozen separate items that he believed he was entitled to. Rodgers categorized the items into two broad groups: (1) items provided to him by the athletic association that were discontinued when he was fired, and (2) items provided by sources other than the athletic association by virtue of his position as head coach.

Specifically, these substantial fringe benefits included the following.

A. Benefits Provided by the Georgia Tech Athletic Association:

- Gas, oil, maintenance, repairs, and other automobile expenses
- Automobile liability and collision insurance
- General expense money
- Meals at the Georgia Tech training table
- Eight season tickets to Georgia Tech home football games
- Two reserved booths (approximately 40 seats) at Georgia Tech home football games
- Six season tickets to Georgia Tech home basketball games
- Four season tickets to Atlanta Falcon home football games
- Four game tickets to out-of-town Georgia Tech football games
- Pocket money at home football games
- Parking privileges at all Georgia Tech home sporting events
- The services of a secretary
- The services of an administrative assistant
- The cost of admission to Georgia Tech home baseball games
- The cost of trips to football coaches' conventions, clinics, and meetings
- Initiation fee, dues, and monthly bills at the Capital City Club
- Initiation fee, dues, and monthly bills at the Cherokee Country Club
- Initiation fee and dues at the East Lake Country Club

B. Benefits from Other Sources:

- Profits from Rodgers's television football show
- Profits from Rodgers's radio football show
- Use of a new Cadillac automobile
- Profits from Rodgers's summer football camp
- Financial gifts from alumni and supporters of Georgia Tech
- Lodging at any of the Holiday Inns owned by Topeka Inn Management, Inc.
- The cost of membership in Terminus International Tennis Club in Atlanta
- Individual game tickets to Hawks basketball and Braves baseball games
- Housing for Rodgers and his family in Atlanta
- The cost of a $400,000 life insurance policy

The pertinent language of the contract provided: "In addition to your salary, as an employee of the Association, you will be entitled to various perquisites as you become eligible therefore." The athletic association contended that the language "as an employee of the Association" limited Rodgers's eligibility for fringe benefits to those items common to all association employees. Rodgers argued that he was entitled to additional benefits as head coach.

The court noted that the contract was drafted by the association, and the record disclosed that Rodgers did in fact receive fringe benefits in addition to those received by other association employees. Accordingly, the court concluded that the parties intended that Rodgers should receive those benefits, as he became eligible therefore, based upon his position as head football coach and not merely as an employee of the association.

Section A Claims

The athletic association asserted that Rodgers was not entitled to any of the items listed in Section A because they were expense account items—"tools" to enable Rodgers to execute his duties as head coach. Rodgers countered that those items were an integral part of his total compensation package and constituted consideration for his contract of employment. The court agreed with the athletic association that Rodgers would be entitled to recover only "compensatory damages." However, three items were in considerable dispute—the services of a secretary, the services of an administrative assistant, and the cost of trips to football conventions and clinics.

The appellate court eventually concluded that the services of the secretary and administrative assistant were intended to assist Rodgers in fulfilling his duties under the contract. Since Rodgers had been relieved of his duties, he had no need for these services. The athletic association was also not obligated to pay his expenses for trips to various football-related activities, since these costs were clearly business-related and not in the nature of compensation.

Section B Claims

The court then turned its attention to those items in Section B— items that Rodgers asserted were fringe benefits that he received from sources other than the athletic association. The athletic association argued that these items were in the nature of tort claims for humiliation and injury to feelings. Rodgers asserted that these items were perquisites that constituted part of the consideration for the contract.

The court did not construe these items to be in the nature of a tort, so it rejected the athletic association's argument. In regard to whether Rodgers could recover the items under a breach of contract theory, the court posed the pertinent question: Can Rodgers's loss of those items be traced to the athletic association's breach of contract?

The record disclosed that the housing expenses and the life insurance premiums were discontinued several years earlier and were not related to the breach of contract. Those items were therefore properly excluded by the trial court. In the eyes of the court, a gift—a voluntary transaction without consideration—could not form an enforceable part of the contract. There was also no evidence that the athletic association had any knowledge of Rodgers's free lodging at certain Holiday Inns or his membership in Terminus International Tennis Club, so those items were excluded.

The unresolved issue was whether the other items—profits from his television and radio shows and from his summer football camp, as well as a new automobile and tickets to professional sporting events—were contemplated by the parties as a probable result of a breach. The court concluded that summary judgment in favor of the athletic association as to these particular fringe benefits was inappropriate. The final resolution of whether Rodgers was entitled to recover those remaining items would have to await a new trial.

The seemingly unlimited perks of a coach, it appeared, were just as fleeting as the rest of life.

Tailgate Time 10

"Blitz" Memphis-Style Dry Ribs

Ingredients

2 racks (about 3 pounds each) of pork spareribs

6 tablespoons kosher salt

2 tablespoons dark brown sugar

1 tablespoon ground black pepper

2 tablespoons paprika

1 tablespoon dried oregano

2 teaspoons garlic powder

1 teaspoon onion powder

1 teaspoon dried thyme

1 teaspoon dried parsley

1 teaspoon ground cumin

1 teaspoon dry mustard powder

½ teaspoon cayenne pepper

¾ cup apple juice

Cooking Instructions

- Mix together sugar, black pepper, paprika, oregano, garlic powder, onion powder, thyme, parsley, cumin, mustard powder, cayenne pepper, and 2 tablespoons of salt.
- Rub pork with all but 2 tablespoons of this spice mixture.

- Mix as basting sauce the remaining 4 tablespoons of salt and 2 tablespoons of spice mixture with apple juice and ¾ cup water in a bowl.
- Prepare grill and place ribs on grate. Baste with sauce, and turn every 20 to 30 minutes until done.

Serves 6

PART III

SPECTATORS

Chapter Eleven

Fall From Grace: The Case of Public Drunkenness

Allen v. Rutgers, State University of New Jersey, 523 A.2d 262 (N.J. 1987)

One fine fall afternoon, Tom Allen and a group of his fraternity brothers excitedly entered the stadium at Rutgers University to watch a football game and participate in an annual frolic known as "Rude Gazer" in which fraternity members, dressed in costume, entered the running track at half-time and ran a quarter-mile race.

In anticipation of the event, Allen and his colleagues managed to consume large quantities of "grain punch," a mixture of fruit punch and 180-proof grain alcohol, which was brought into the stadium in five- and ten-gallon containers, in spite of the university policy prohibiting the consumption of alcoholic beverages at such events.

Not surprisingly, Allen became progressively intoxicated as he drank the potent elixir, even to the extent of falling asleep. At one point, Allen stumbled into the arms of a security officer, which prompted the other members of the group to quickly get him back to his seat. One of the ushers, noticing the scene, recommended that Allen be taken home.

Eventually, Allen and several of his more peripatetic colleagues moved into a grassy bluff area. The group then proceeded to the opposite side of the stadium. In a burst of enthusiasm, Allen rushed to the top of the stands and vaulted over the wall—not realizing there was a 30-foot drop to the concrete steps below. Not surprisingly, Allen sustained severe and permanent injuries as a result.

With no one else to blame, Allen proceeded to sue the university. The jury quickly determined that the university's negligence was *not* the proximate cause of his injuries. Allen moved for a new trial because the judge refused to remove evidence of his intoxication.

Allen's argument to the court—incredibly enough—was (1) that by adopting policies relating to alcoholic beverages, the university assumed the duty of protecting a person in Allen's condition against subjecting *himself* to injury, and (2) that this duty could not be mitigated by the very conduct it was intended to prevent—intoxication. The trial judge was either not amused or not persuaded by the plaintiff's novel argument, and he permitted the jury to consider evidence of Allen's comparative negligence.

Allen insisted his negligence should not have been submitted to the jury, as he was a member of the class protected by the university policy against the use of alcoholic beverages. Allen analogized the situation to dram shop cases. Thus, he argued, the anti-alcohol rules of the university created a *duty* to protect those attending a football game—including inebriates—from dangerous situations related to the consumption of alcohol. Allen urged that the university's breach of its self-imposed standards of conduct eliminated comparative negligence as a defense in the same way that service of liquor to a visibly intoxicated patron or guest would in other contexts.

The court was unmoved by Allen's argument. Implementation of the university's no-alcohol rule may have had the effect of protecting patrons against their own folly, but it did not render the university liable for injuries resulting from its violation. Placing the university in the same category as a tavern owner or social host who provided liquor to an intoxicated person was "factually unwarranted and legally unjustified."

The court concluded that it was within the province of the jury to determine whether Allen's injuries were proximately related to the negligence of the university. The jury was apparently so offended by Allen's crass behavior that it refused to reward him a single cent for his improvident leap over the wall.

Frankly, it was a reaction that is difficult to find fault with.

"Throw the Pigskin" Grilled Pork Sandwiches

Ingredients

2 pork tenderloins (about ¾ pound)

1 teaspoon garlic powder

1 teaspoon dry mustard

1 teaspoon salt

½ teaspoon ground pepper

vegetable oil

6 tablespoons vidalia onion barbecue sauce

6 hamburger buns

Cooking Instructions

- Mix together garlic powder, mustard, salt, and pepper.
- Rub pork tenderloins evenly with garlic powder mixture, and then lightly coat with vegetable oil.
- Grill pork over medium-high heat about 10 minutes on each side.
- Drizzle with vidalia onion barbecue sauce.
- Chop or slice pork tenderloins, and serve on hamburger buns.

Serves 6

Chapter Twelve

Flying Objects: The Duty to Protect

Hayden v. University of Notre Dame, 716
N.E.2d 603 (Ind. App. 1999)

Season ticket holders DeWilliam and Letitia Hayden were happily attending a football game on the Notre Dame campus when an accident occurred.

The Haydens sat in their reserved seats in the south end zone, and during the second quarter, one of the teams kicked the football toward the goal. The net behind the goal posts failed to stop the ball, and it landed in the stands close to Letitia Hayden. Several fans in the crowd lunged for the ball in an effort to retrieve it as a souvenir, and one of these individuals struck Hayden from behind, forcefully knocking her to the ground and injuring her shoulder.

No doubt assuming that the young hoodlum was judgment proof, Mrs. Hayden sued the university for failing to exercise due care to protect her from injury. The trial court granted the university's motion for summary judgment, reasoning that the university did not have a legal duty to prevent such consequences. Hayden's appeal posed but one issue for review: Did the trial court err in concluding that Notre Dame did not owe a duty to Hayden to protect her from the criminal acts of a third party?

Hayden argued that this case was governed by premises liability principles and that the relevant standard of care was determined by her status as a business invitee. The university did not dispute Hayden's status, but it did deny that it owed any duty to protect her from the criminal act of a third party. The university contended that the incident was unforeseeable, and that it had no obligation to anticipate it and protect people against it.

In determining when a landowner must take reasonable precautions to prevent foreseeable criminal actions against invitees, the court followed the "totality of the circumstances" test. The court explained that it must consider all of the circumstances surrounding an event (including the nature, condition, and location of the premises), as well as prior incidents, to determine whether a criminal act was foreseeable.

Applying this test to the case before it, the court found that Notre Dame *should* have foreseen that injury could result from the actions of a third party in lunging for the ball after it landed in the stands. The court remarked that Notre Dame well understood—and greatly benefited from—the enthusiasm of its fans. In fact, it was such emotion that drove some of these aficionados to make wild attempts at grabbing errant footballs.

There was evidence of many prior incidents of spectators being jostled or injured by those attempting to retrieve a ball. Hayden testified that she and her husband frequently witnessed people striving to retrieve footballs landing in their vicinity, and that she had previously been knocked off her seat by such an attempt. Hayden estimated that the goal post net caught the ball only about half the time.

Based on the totality of the circumstances, the trial court held that Notre Dame *did* owe Hayden a duty to take reasonable steps to protect her from injury. Whether such steps included a requirement that in the future spectators wear football helmets was not discussed.

Tailgate Time 12

"Line of Scrimmage" Beef Fajitas

Ingredients

2 pounds of flank steak

¼ cup fresh lime juice

4 cloves garlic, peeled and smashed

2 tablespoons cilantro leaves, chopped

2 teaspoons Worcestershire sauce

1 teaspoon dried oregano, crushed

1 teaspoon red pepper flakes

1 teaspoon ground cumin

1 teaspoon ground coriander

2 tablespoons vegetable oil

2 teaspoons salt

1 teaspoon ground black pepper

6 large flour tortillas

1 red bell pepper, thinly sliced

1 green bell pepper, thinly sliced

1 yellow bell pepper, thinly sliced

1 large white onion, thinly sliced

1 tablespoon minced garlic

Lime wedges

Cooking Instructions

- In a bowl, mix together the lime juice, garlic, cilantro, Worcestershire sauce, oregano, pepper flakes, cumin, coriander, and 1 tablespoon of the vegetable oil. Pour into a large zip-lock bag, add the steak, and seal. Refrigerate for at least 12 hours, turning occasionally.
- Remove meat from the bag, and season on both sides with 1 teaspoon of salt and ½ teaspoon of black pepper.
- Preheat grill to high, and preheat oven to 325° F.
- Wrap tortillas in foil and place in oven for 15 minutes to warm and soften. Remove and keep warm in aluminum foil.
- Cook steak over grill to preference.
- In large skillet, heat remaining vegetable oil over medium-high heat. Add bell peppers and onions, and cook about 15 minutes. Add garlic, remaining teaspoon of salt, and ½ teaspoon of pepper and cook for 1 to 2 minutes.
- Thinly slice the steak. Divide among the warmed tortillas and top with the vegetables. Drizzle with lime juice.

Serves 6

Chapter Thirteen

Defective Goal Post: Waiver of Governmental Immunity

University of Texas v. Moreno, 172 S.W.3d 281 (Tex. App.—El Paso 2005)

Sometimes postgame celebrations on the football field can get a little out of hand.

Gabriel Moreno was attending a game at the University of Texas at El Paso stadium (commonly known as the Sun Bowl) when the UTEP team he came to support reigned victorious. In a burst of enthusiasm, many of the attendees—including Moreno himself—streamed wildly onto the field. Moreno was hanging from the top of the goal post when some of the other rabble-rousers began to tear it down. Moreno, not surprisingly, was injured in the process.

What was more surprising was that Moreno filed suit against the university for his injuries. Initially, the controlling issue was whether the Texas Tort Claims Act waived immunity for the personal injuries suffered by Moreno, who alleged that (1) the goal post constituted a premises defect liability, and (2) the university failed to erect barriers to control the postgame crowd.

UTEP maintained that as a governmental unit it was immune from suit unless the Tort Claims Act specifically waived that immunity, and that Moreno's claims did not allege a true premises defect that would permit such a suit.

The court astutely observed that Moreno's allegations of negligence did not concern a defect in the premises, but were instead related to overzealous fans knocking down a goal post. Nothing in the plaintiff's petition revealed how the goal post itself was "defective." Moreno conceded in his deposition that he was basically suing the university for its failure to control the crowd.

Moreno then—conveniently enough—amended his petition to contend that UTEP was negligent in failing to install goal posts that were free from defects. Still, the real substance of his claim was that UTEP was liable for the out-of-control tortious conduct of individuals seeking to destroy university property.

The court was not sympathetic. A cause of action based on the negligent use of real property does not exist separately from a cause of action for a premises defect, and in the eyes of the court, Moreno had not stated a cause of action for a premises defect because he had not alleged a physical imperfection that was the proximate cause of his injuries.

Despite Moreno's statements that the goal post was defective, the deposition testimony and pleadings established that the only complaint about the goal posts was that they were torn down by an unruly crowd. Such an allegation did not satisfy the waiver of sovereign immunity under the act where the *condition* of the property itself must have caused the injury. The court noted that the property did not cause the injury if it did no more than furnish the condition that made the injury possible.

Moreno also complained that university personnel had a duty to control the crowd through the use of barriers, gates, link chains, and security devices, and that its failure to do so was negligent. The court did not agree. The injuries Moreno suffered were the result of criminal acts of third parties, and the court remained firm that a governmental entity was exempt from liability for intentional torts "arising out of assault, battery, false imprisonment, or any other intentional tort."

In the view of the court, Moreno complained of injuries that occurred because of deliberately destructive behavior of the crowd—behavior that, the court astutely noted, included that of Moreno himself. Denying relief, the court gave Moreno something to think about the next time he hung precariously from a goal post in a fit of blissful revelry.

"Extra Point" Meatball Sandwiches

Ingredients
3 hoagie buns
⅓ cup butter, softened
1 teaspoon garlic powder
¼ teaspoon salt (or to taste)
black pepper (to taste)
1 14-ounce can spaghetti sauce
6 slices mozzarella cheese

For Meatballs
1 pound ground beef
¼ cup milk
1 egg, slightly beaten
1 tablespoon fresh garlic, minced
¼ cup parmesan cheese, grated
1 egg, slightly beaten
2 teaspoons seasoned salt
½ teaspoon black pepper
2 tablespoons fresh parsley, chopped
⅓ cup breadcrumbs

Cooking Instructions

- For the meatballs: in a large bowl mix all ingredients listed, and shape into a dozen meatballs. Place on a baking sheet, and bake at 350° F. for about 30 minutes.
- Cut hoagie buns in half and remove some of the bread from the inside to accommodate meatballs.
- In a small bowl, mix the softened butter with garlic powder and ¼ teaspoon salt; spread over the inside slices of bread; then sprinkle with black pepper to taste.
- Bake bread until lightly toasted.
- In a medium saucepan warm the pasta sauce over medium heat.
- When the meatballs are cooked, add them into the sauce.
- Spoon the sauce and meatballs over bread, then top with mozzarella cheese slices.

Serves 6

Chapter Fourteen

Bleacher Collapse: The Doctrine of Charitable Immunity

Southern Methodist University v. Clayton,
176 S.W.2d 749 (Tex. 1944)

In the midst of a spirited football game one beautiful autumnal afternoon on the leafy campus of Southern Methodist University (which happened to be playing Texas A&M that day), a very unfortunate thing occurred—a temporary bleacher collapsed.

Mrs. J. B. Clayton was firmly ensconced in the stands when it fell violently to the ground. Sustaining substantial injuries, she filed suit against the university to recover her damages. She alleged that the university was negligent in several respects: (1) permitting the stand to be crowded beyond its capacity, (2) failing to sufficiently support the stand with braces, (3) constructing the stand of old and defective material, and (4) negligently hiring a grounds supervisor named L. B. Morgan, who, Clayton claimed, was incompetent. During trial, she dropped the fourth allegation concerning the negligent hiring of Mr. Morgan.

The university moved for an instructed verdict, and the trial court sustained its motion. Clayton appealed, and the trial court's ruling was eventually reversed and remanded by the Court of Civil

Appeals. The university then brought this appeal to the Texas Supreme Court.

In its decision, the Supreme Court recognized that SMU, as an institution of higher learning, was benevolent and charitable in character, having no capital stock or stockholders. The court also observed that since Clayton had abandoned her allegation of negligence in the employment of Morgan, there was no basis on which the jury could determine that the university was liable.

The court noted that there was a wide divergence of authority among the various jurisdictions as to the tort liability of charitable institutions, depending upon whether the plaintiff was a beneficiary or a stranger. Some jurisdictions extended absolute immunity, others recognized limited liability, and a few followed the doctrine of respondeat superior, in which the institution could be held liable to a stranger who proved negligence, proximate cause, and damages.

The court remarked that in Texas it was well established that a charity *was* liable for injuries caused by the negligence of the charity's officers, vice principals, or agents. On the other hand, it was equally well settled that a charity was *not* liable for injuries to its *beneficiaries*, provided it was not negligent in hiring the employee whose actions caused the injuries. Whether the nonliability rule should be extended to *strangers* was the unsettled question before the court.

Clayton contended that (1) she was on the university's campus as a guest paying to watch a football game, (2) she was a stranger to the university's charitable purpose of promoting education, and (3) she was therefore entitled to damages for injuries sustained. Clayton conceded that if she had been a *student* (i.e., a beneficiary), the university would *not* have been liable unless it had been negligent in the hiring of Morgan.

After analyzing the situation, the court could see no basis for the distinction between beneficiaries and strangers. The court reasoned that the exemption of charities from tort actions rested not on the relation of the injured person to the charity, but on public policy, which forbid punishing charities in order to compensate members of the public for injuries resulting from the negligence of the charity. The rights of the individual were subordinate to the public good on the assumption that it was preferable the individual suffer injury without compensation than for the public to be deprived of the charity's benefit.

To hold SMU liable would have reduced the size of its general fund, which would otherwise be devoted to its charitable purpose. Finding liability would have deprived the public of these charitable activities, and the principle of respondeat superior would impair the university. The fact that SMU's football program was not financially self-sustaining further reinforced this conclusion.

As a result, the Supreme Court felt that sound public policy demanded that charitable institutions be held immune from liability for their agents' torts in the absence of negligence in employing them—regardless of whether the injured party was a beneficiary or a stranger—since the end result to the charity was the same.

The still injured—and now uncompensated—Mrs. Clayton no doubt had other thoughts on the matter.

"Hail Mary" Fried Chicken

Ingredients

1 3-pound whole chicken, cut into pieces
1 cup flour
salt
ground black pepper
1 teaspoon paprika
1 quart vegetable oil

Cooking Instructions

- Season chicken pieces with salt, pepper, and paprika. Roll in flour.
- Add oil to a large, heavy skillet to a level of ½ to ¾ inch. Heat to approximately 350° F.
- Place chicken pieces in hot oil. Cover, and fry until golden, about 15 to 20 minutes.

Serves 6

PART IV

NCAA

Chapter Fifteen

Stringent Sanctions: The Constitutional Challenge

Justice v. NCAA, 577 F.Supp. 356 (D. Ariz. 1983)

No one likes sanctions, least of all those who did absolutely nothing to deserve them.

The plaintiffs in this lawsuit were football players at the University of Arizona who urged that a preliminary injunction be issued against the NCAA to prevent sanctions that rendered their team ineligible for two years to either participate in postseason competition or to make television appearances. The players and coaches whose actions brought about the sanctions were, of course, long gone.

The report of the NCAA Infractions Committee documented numerous occasions in which staff members of the UA football program (including the head coach) provided compensation—airline tickets, lodging, cash, and bank loans—to players and recruits. Neither the university nor the players denied these allegations.

In their complaint in federal court, the plaintiffs alleged that the NCAA's sanctions deprived them of their constitutionally protected rights:

- to be free of punishment in the absence of guilt,
- to participate in intercollegiate athletic competition (including postseason bowl games) and thereby receive national exposure critical to securing a professional football contract, and
- to pursue the vocation of their choice and to exercise their freedom of expression without prior restraints.

The plaintiffs further alleged that sanctions imposed by an association consisting of universities that were in competition with the University of Arizona constituted a group boycott in violation of the Sherman Act. The plaintiffs also contended that by precluding them from competing with other highly rated football teams in postseason play, and that by denying them the exposure necessary to compete for contracts and bonuses with professional football teams upon graduation, the sanctions would cause immediate and irreparable harm if not corrected before postseason bowl game invitations. As their remedy, the plaintiffs sought a preliminary injunction prohibiting the NCAA from implementing the sanctions.

Free from Punishment

The players asserted that the sanctions had infringed their fundamental right to be free from punishment, absent personal guilt. None of the players or coaching staff at that time had been involved in the violations for which the sanctions were imposed. The NCAA argued that the broad principle of freedom from punishment was not applicable in the instant case because there had been no deprivation of property or liberty that was protected by the constitution.

The court agreed that it was unfortunate that the players were innocent of the wrongdoing that led to the sanctions, but it concluded that the situation did not elevate the interest to a constitutional right protected by the due process clause of the Fourteenth Amendment. The court noted that sanctions that effectively punished innocent athletes for the conduct of others were not uncommon in the sports world, and the only question was whether the NCAA's action was so irrational that it could be deemed arbitrary.

The court concluded that the sanctions imposed by the NCAA were not arbitrary or irrational. The promotion of amateurism in intercollegiate athletics is a legitimate objective of the NCAA, and sanctions against universities for compensating athletes are rationally related to the NCAA's objectives. The sanctions imposed in this case were directed against specific misconduct by the University of Arizona. They served to deter the university and other member institutions from engaging in similar activities, and they were meant to deny the university the benefits derived from its improper practices. The interests of current players in participating in postseason and televised football contests had to be subordinated to the NCAA's broader interests in preserving the amateur nature of the sport.

Constitutional Violations

In their lawsuit, the players first contended that as recipients of athletic scholarships they possessed constitutionally protected contractual property interests in playing in bowl games and appearing on television. The court observed that in order to have a property interest, a person must have more than unilateral expectation of it—he must have a legitimate *entitlement* to it.

In that light, the court found that the players had not been deprived of their scholarships nor their right to participate in intercollegiate athletics. Whatever oral representations were made about postseason and televised athletic contests created a mere *expectation*, not a legitimate claim of entitlement based on contract.

The players' second argument asserted a constitutionally protected right to participate in intercollegiate athletics—including televised and postseason bowl game competitions—which had been infringed without due process of law. The court was mindful of the Supreme Court's directive that in order for procedural due process guarantees to be invoked, there must be a denial of a right previously recognized by state law. The Arizona courts—unfortunately for the players—had not recognized participation in intercollegiate competition as a protectable property right.

The district court decided that it need not address the question of whether the players had a protectable property interest because the NCAA sanctions deprived the players of no such interest: the plaintiffs continued to participate in regular season competition. The real question was whether there was a constitutional property right that protected postseason competition and television appearances. The court likewise found no such property or liberty interests of which the plaintiffs had been deprived.

The players' third theory was that they had a protected interest in receiving national exposure critical to obtaining a contract with a professional football team. The court remarked that this property interest was even more attenuated than the first two. The court did not deny that bowl competition and televised games could have an impact on a player's salary in the professional ranks, but it flatly rejected the assertion that the players had a constitutional right to such.

Other Constitutional Claims

The players alleged two additional constitutional violations. First, they claimed that the action of the NCAA had interfered with their rights to pursue the vocation of their choosing, which was based upon the liberty and property concepts of the due process clause. The court dismissed this claim, noting that case law clearly rejected the notion that student-athletes' expectations of future athletic careers were constitutionally protected.

Second, the players contended that the NCAA's denial of television coverage of postseason bowl competition constituted a prior restraint upon the First Amendment's freedom of expression. They claimed, first, that their own right to expression through entertainment was being unreasonably restricted, and second, that millions of individuals across the country who watched football had been denied their right to entertainment.

In analyzing these claims, the court noted that in its most basic form, athletic competition did not constitute pure speech, but was rather a physical activity that was not constitutionally protected. The court also dismissed the notion that the NCAA sanctions denied the public at large its right to entertainment because there is no protectable, legitimate form of expression in playing college football.

Antitrust Issues

The players alleged that the NCAA's imposition of the sanctions constituted an unreasonable restraint of trade under the Sherman Act. In particular, the players contended that the sanctions that excluded the team from postseason and televised competition constituted an agreement to prevent the university from reaching consumers, and thus were a per se illegal group boycott.

The NCAA responded with the following: (1) the players had not suffered an "antitrust injury" sufficient to entitle them to relief, (2) the Sherman Act was not applicable because the sanctions did not affect "trade" or "commerce," (3) the NCAA procedure did not have an anticompetitive purpose but rather promoted the goals of a private sports association, and (4) the sanctions were a reasonable restraint under the rule of reason.

The court explained that the Sherman Act did not prohibit all concerted actions or agreements—only those that unreasonably restrained trade. In this case, the attributes of a per se illegal boycott simply did not exist. There was concerted activity only in the sense that the NCAA was a membership organization enforcing its rules, and the regulations at issue pertained solely to the association's goal of preserving amateurism. There was no showing by the players that the NCAA, its member institutions, or the Infractions Committee had any purpose to insulate themselves from competition by imposing sanctions on the University of Arizona or any of the other universities on probation.

The sanctions against the University of Arizona—harsh as they no doubt appeared—would therefore remain firmly in place.

Tailgate Time 15

"Home Field Advantage" Sloppy Joes

Ingredients

1 pound lean ground beef

¼ cup onion, chopped

¼ cup green bell pepper, chopped

½ teaspoon garlic powder

1 teaspoon yellow mustard

¾ cup ketchup

3 teaspoons brown sugar

salt to taste

ground black pepper to taste

Cooking Instructions

- In medium-sized skillet over medium heat, brown the ground beef, onion, and green pepper; drain off liquids.
- Stir in garlic powder, mustard, ketchup, and brown sugar; mix thoroughly. Reduce heat, and simmer for 30 minutes. Season with salt and pepper.

Serves 6

Chapter Sixteen

Television Time: Antitrust Ramifications

NCAA v. University of Oklahoma, 468 U.S. 85 (1984)

It seemed like a good idea at the time—until the United States Supreme Court got involved.

In 1981 the NCAA adopted a plan for the televising of football games of its member institutions for the 1982–1985 seasons. The restrictions were intended to reduce the adverse effect of live television on football game attendance by limiting the number of games that a university could televise. No member of the NCAA was permitted to make a sale of television rights except in accordance with the plan.

The NCAA had separate agreements with two networks—ABC and CBS—granting each the right to telecast the games described in the plan. Each network agreed to pay a specified amount to NCAA members, and each network was allowed to negotiate directly with the universities for the right to televise their games.

The University of Oklahoma and the University of Georgia were also members of the College Football Association (CFA), whose high-profile members claimed they should have a greater voice in the formulation of television policy than they possessed in the NCAA.

The CFA negotiated a contract with NBC that allowed a greater number of television appearances and therefore increased the revenues of its members. The NCAA announced that it would take disciplinary action against any CFA member that complied with the CFA–NBC contract. As a result, the University of Oklahoma and the University of Georgia filed an action against the NCAA.

The district court found that the NCAA regulations violated the Sherman Act, and that competition in the relevant market—defined as "live college football television"—had been restrained in three ways: (1) the NCAA fixed the price for particular telecasts, (2) its exclusive network contracts were tantamount to a group boycott of all other broadcasters, and (3) its plan placed an artificial limit on the production of televised college football.

"In a competitive market," the district court observed, "each football-playing institution would be an independent seller of the right to telecast its football games." Each seller would be free to sell that right "to any entity it chose" and "for whatever price it could get." Under the NCAA's plan, this competitive freedom was restrained because television rights were bought and sold as a package deal rather than on a per-game basis.

The district court held that the plan constituted price fixing and output limitation, which were illegal per se under the Sherman Act. The court also held that the scheme was an illegal group boycott, a forbidden monopolization, and an unreasonable restraint of trade. The court entered an injunction against the NCAA.

The NCAA appealed. The Court of Appeals, while disagreeing with the boycott and monopolization holdings, otherwise upheld the district court's judgment that the television plan violated the Sherman Act, and it focused almost entirely on the price-fixing and output-limiting aspects of the television plan. The NCAA appealed again, this time to the U.S. Supreme Court.

The Supreme Court concluded that the NCAA's television plan did in fact violate the Sherman Act. While the television plan had sufficient redeeming virtues to escape condemnation as a per se violation of the Sherman Act, the NCAA plan was an unreasonable restraint of trade because of its price-fixing and output-limiting characteristics. In the Court's mind, there was no doubt that the practices of the NCAA constituted a restraint of trade in the sense that they limited members' freedom to enter into their own television contracts. By preventing member institutions from competing against each other on the basis of price or type of television rights, the NCAA had created a horizontal restraint—an agreement among competitors about the way they could compete with one another. Because it placed a ceiling on the number of games, the horizontal agreement placed an artificial limit on the quantity of televised football that was available to broadcasters and consumers. By restraining the quantity of television rights available for sale, the NCAA created a limitation on output that was thus an unreasonable restraint of trade.

The anticompetitive consequences of this arrangement were apparent. Individual competitors lost their freedom to compete, and the price was higher and the output lower than they otherwise would have been. The NCAA clearly possessed market power. College football telecasts generated an audience uniquely attractive to advertisers, and competitors were unable to offer programming that attracted a similar audience. The NCAA's control over those broadcasts revealed that the NCAA possessed market power with respect to those broadcasts. The Court found that the fact that more games would be televised in a free market was reason enough to reject the NCAA plan.

There was, however, a vigorous dissent, which maintained that the primary goal of the NCAA was to maintain a clear line of demarcation between college athletics and professional sports. In pursuit of that goal, the NCAA imposed controls on competition that would be condemned if undertaken in a traditional business setting. Yet each of these regulations represented a legitimate attempt to keep university athletics from becoming professionalized to the extent that profit-making objectives would overshadow educational objectives. In the minds of the dissenters, the NCAA television plan did not differ fundamentally from the other seemingly anticompetitive aspects of the organization's broader program of self-regulation. The television plan was designed to (1) reduce the adverse effects of television on football game attendance and, in turn, promote the athletic and related educational programs that were dependent upon the resulting revenue, (2) preserve amateurism, and (3) integrate athletics and education.

The minority opinion saw the television plan as eminently reasonable because it fostered amateurism by spreading revenues among various schools and reducing financial incentives toward professionalism. In its view, the restrictions of the television plan were entirely consistent with the overall objectives of the NCAA.

Tailgate Time 16

"Backfield in Motion" Beer Brats

Ingredients

6 bratwurst sausages
2 teaspoons butter
1 large sweet onion, thinly sliced
6 ounces of beer

Cooking Instructions

- Heat 1 teaspoon of butter in heavy cookware. Brown bratwurst sausages until deep golden brown. Remove to a platter.
- To the drippings, add the remaining teaspoon of butter and the onion slices. Cook, stirring often, until onions are golden but not brown.
- Return bratwurst to the onions and add the beer. Cook over medium heat about 15 minutes, turning midway through.

Serves 6

Chapter Seventeen

The No-Draft Rule: Preserving Amateur Status

Banks v. NCAA, 977 F.2d 1081 (7th Cir. 1992)

The best laid plans of an aspiring professional athlete can sometimes go horribly awry.

Braxston Banks entered Notre Dame on a full football scholarship, and as a freshman, he played in all 11 games. In the first game of his sophomore year, he injured his knee, and he saw play in only seven games. In his junior year, that number diminished to six games. Banks then chose to sit out his senior year to allow his knee to fully recover. Having competed for three years, he was eligible to enter the National Football League draft, and so he did.

Banks's plan was based partially on a fear that another season of college football might expose him to further injury and thus prevent him from entering the pros. As news of Banks's entrance into the draft became public, virtually every NFL team was interested, and representatives visited Notre Dame and put him through efficiency drills to test his skills. Banks also participated in an NFL tryout in Indianapolis, but he performed poorly and was not selected in the draft or as a free agent.

Under the NCAA rules, an athlete is eligible to play four seasons of an intercollegiate sport within five years of commencing his college education. Because he sat out his senior year, Banks had one year of intercollegiate eligibility remaining when he graduated. Even though he was exposing himself to further injury, he decided that the only way to demonstrate his ability to compete on the professional level was to return to Notre Dame for graduate courses and reenter the football program during his final year of eligibility.

Unfortunately for Banks, two NCAA eligibility rules stood in his way:

- the no-draft rule, which provided that a player loses his amateur status when he is placed on the draft list of a professional league, and
- the no-agent rule, which provided that a player is ineligible for participation in an intercollegiate sport if he is represented by a sports agent.

Since Banks participated in the draft tryouts and was represented by an agent, either of the two rules was sufficient to bar him from participating in his final year of eligibility at Notre Dame.

The Notre Dame coaches apparently wanted Banks to play, but because no college had ever appealed to the NCAA to restore eligibility of a player who had entered the NFL draft, the university refused to request that the NCAA reinstate him. With Notre Dame's football season rapidly approaching, Banks filed his complaint in federal district court, contending that the NCAA rules violated the antitrust laws by restricting opportunities in the labor market for collegiate football players. Banks also suggested that the rules effected a group boycott by the NCAA and the NFL. Banks, however, failed to describe exactly what anticompetitive effects resulted from either restraint. The court therefore held that Banks failed to show an adverse market impact.

On appeal, Banks alleged that the NCAA no-draft and no-agent rules restrained trade in three ways:

- NCAA universities were restricted from offering a player such as Banks an opportunity to play college football again. The relevant market was made up of all those players who wished to play football for major college football teams, which was dominated by the NCAA.
- All members of the NCAA were required to abide by its rules, and this restraint operated indirectly, although intentionally, on players such as Banks.
- The ability of a player such as Banks to market his services to the NFL was prohibited by giving him only one realistic chance to be drafted by the NFL. The market being restrained was made up of players like Banks who considered entering the NFL draft while they still had college football eligibility remaining.

The appellate court failed to see how the NCAA no-draft rules had an anticompetitive impact on the college football labor market. In its view, the NCAA rules sought to promote fair amateur competition, encourage the educational pursuits of student-athletes, prevent commercialism, and retain a clear line of demarcation between intercollegiate athletics and professional sports. The no-draft rule had no more impact than other NCAA eligibility requirements such as those pertaining to grades, semester hours, or the acquisition of a high school diploma. They all constituted eligibility requirements essential to participation in NCAA-sponsored amateur athletic competitions.

The NCAA rules did not restrain trade, the court concluded, because the NCAA did not exist as a minor league training ground for future NFL players. In the eyes of the majority of the court, the no-agent and no-draft rules were vital to preserve the amateur status of college athletics and to prevent sports agents from invading the system.

A vigorous dissent disagreed. It contended that NCAA member colleges were the purchasers of labor in this market, and that the players were the suppliers. The players agreed to compete in football games that typically earned the colleges a profit in exchange for tuition, room, board, and other benefits.

In the view of the dissent, the NCAA rules harmed competition in the market: they foreclosed players from choosing a major college football team based on the willingness of the institution to waive the rule. The no-draft rule eliminated this element of competition among colleges, who were the purchasers of labor in the college football market. The rule categorically ruled out a term of employment that players—the suppliers of labor in that market—would find advantageous.

The dissent snidely remarked that the "gentlemen's agreement" between the NFL and the college powers kept all but a handful of players from turning pro before their four-year period of "servitude" was completed:

> The pros get a free farm system that supplies them with well-trained, much publicized employees. The colleges get to keep their players the equivalent of barefoot and pregnant.

That really smarts.

Tailgate Time 17

"Field Goal" Jalapeno Cornbread

Ingredients
¾ cup flour
¾ cup yellow cornmeal
¼ cup sugar
1½ teaspoons salt
1½ teaspoons baking powder
1 teaspoon baking soda
½ cup green onions, sliced
2 teaspoons jalapenos, minced
1¼ cups buttermilk
2 large eggs
¼ cup butter, melted

Cooking Instructions
- Preheat oven to 350° F.
- Butter a 13 × 9 × 2-inch baking pan.
- Whisk together flour, cornmeal, sugar, salt, baking powder, and baking soda in a large bowl to blend.
- Stir in green onions and jalapenos.
- Whisk together buttermilk and eggs in a medium bowl to blend, then whisk in melted butter.

Tailgate Time 17 (continued)

- Add buttermilk mixture to dry ingredients and stir.
- Transfer batter to buttered pan.
- Bake for 20–30 minutes, or until golden brown.

Serves 6

Chapter Eighteen

Human Billboards: Regulating Uniform Logos

Adidas America v. NCAA, 40 F.Supp.2d 1275 (D. Kan. 1999)

Manufacturers of athletic apparel must walk a fine line to keep from running afoul of NCAA rules on illegal advertising.

NCAA Bylaw 12.5.5 seeks to limit the size of advertising logos permitted on athletes' uniforms used during competition. Specifically, this bylaw provides (a) that athletics equipment "shall bear only the manufacturer's normal label or trademark, as it is used on such items for sale to the general public," and (b) that an athlete's apparel "shall bear only a single manufacturer's or distributor's normal label or trademark not to exceed 2¼ square inches in area."

The NCAA had repeatedly determined that the distinctive Adidas trademark—consisting of three descending stripes down the sleeve or pant leg—was the equivalent of a logo as defined by the bylaw. Any Adidas uniform bearing a three-stripe design element larger than two and one-quarter square inches was in violation.

To enjoin the NCAA from enforcing its Bylaw 12.5.5, Adidas filed suit for injunctive relief under violations of the Sherman Act, as well as state law claims of tortious interference with contractual relations and breach of contract, among others.

Adidas had been down this road before. The Adidas "Velez" jersey, for example, was initially deemed compliant and then later held to be in violation when it was determined that its striped design elements resembled the company's trademark. In another case, Adidas submitted a size medium "Team Stripe" jersey to the NCAA for approval. The sleeve of the jersey had only two stripes, so the NCAA concluded that it complied with the bylaw. When the jersey was later viewed by the NCAA in a size large, it was deemed in violation because the additional sleeve material in the larger size caused a third stripe to appear. Those clever designers at Adidas were clearly a force to be reckoned with.

Due to numerous adverse rulings, Adidas claimed that Bylaw 12.5.5 was illegal and that the NCAA was applying the bylaw unfairly. NCAA's general counsel offered to provide Adidas with an NCAA staff member who would review the company's proposed production line and give definitive answers as to whether particular designs violated the bylaw. Adidas declined to accept the offer.

The purpose of the bylaw, the NCAA claimed, was to preserve the integrity of college athletics and to avoid the commercial exploitation of student-athletes. Furthermore, the bylaw was designed to avoid excessive advertising that could interfere with the basic function of the uniforms, which was to provide identification of the athlete. There was no commercial purpose behind the creation and enforcement of the bylaw. Neither the NCAA nor its member institutions obtained any economic or competitive advantage against Adidas or other apparel manufacturers.

The court therefore concluded that Adidas had failed to establish its right to preliminary injunctive relief. Specifically, Adidas had failed to show that it faced irreparable harm or that there was a likelihood that it would eventually prevail on the merits of its claims.

Irreparable Harm

Adidas claimed that without an injunction it would suffer a diminution of its intellectual property, as well as injury to its reputation, its relationships with member institutions, its processing and manufacturing partners, and the buying public. However, the company offered only conjecture to establish its irreparable injury, and the court found such evidence to be insufficient.

Adidas then presented evidence that the NCAA applied the bylaw in an inconsistent and unpredictable fashion. However, the company failed to show that the NCAA's application was intentional or that it resulted in irreparable harm. The court concluded that any harm could be compensated by monetary damages.

The court also noted that Adidas had placed itself in harm's way. Adidas could have submitted its designs to the NCAA for prior approval. Had Adidas attempted to comply with the bylaw prior to litigation, it might have increased its design and production costs, but it could have avoided the alleged irreparable effects on its business, profits, and reputation. Even if the court were to conclude that the bylaw was illegal or arbitrarily applied, an injunction was inappropriate because any harm resulted from the company's willful failure to comply with the bylaw.

Likelihood of Success

Adidas claimed that the NCAA had unreasonably restrained trade and engaged in a group boycott in violation of section 1 of the

Sherman Act, and had attempted to monopolize in violation of section 2 of the act. Adidas also alleged interference with contractual relations, interference with prospective economic advantage, breach of contract, and violations of NCAA bylaws and rules and public policy. The court concluded that Adidas failed to establish a likelihood that it would prevail on the merits of its federal or state law claims.

The NCAA argued that, for antitrust purposes, Bylaw 12.5.5 was indistinguishable from its noncommercial eligibility rules and should not be subject to Sherman Act scrutiny because the bylaw, like the eligibility rules, had neither the purpose nor the effect of giving the NCAA or its member institutions an advantage in any commercial transaction. The court agreed.

On its face, the bylaw set standards on uniforms, equipment, and other apparel worn by student-athletes in NCAA competition. To determine whether the bylaw was commercial, the court had to examine the underlying purposes of the bylaw, the NCAA's reasons for creating the advertising regulation, and whether the bylaw conferred a direct economic benefit on the NCAA.

The court concluded that the purpose of the bylaw was threefold:

- to maintain amateurism by protecting student-athletes from commercial exploitation,
- to preserve the integrity of intercollegiate sports by preventing member schools from turning their student-athletes into advertising billboards, and
- to avoid excessive advertising that could potentially interfere with the basic function of uniforms, which was to provide identification of the athlete to his teammates and to the referee officiating the contest.

Holding that the NCAA's enforcement of the bylaw was a non-commercial activity not subject to antitrust laws, the court sent Adidas back to the drawing board—from whence creative ways of circumventing the restrictions of the now-suspicious regulators would no doubt soon appear.

Tailgate Time 18

"End Zone" Brownies

Ingredients

1 cup butter

2 cups white sugar

½ cup cocoa powder

1 teaspoon vanilla extract

4 eggs

1½ cups flour

½ teaspoon baking powder

½ teaspoon salt

½ cup walnut halves

Cooking Instructions

- Melt the butter and mix it together with all ingredients above.
- Bake at 350° F. for about 30 minutes in a 9 × 13-inch greased pan.

Serves 6

Afterword

O'Bannon v. NCAA

College sports—and particularly the revenue-producing sports like football—are a dynamic world, and as this book is going to press (August 2014), a federal judge has turned that universe upside down, ruling in the antitrust case of *O'Bannon v. NCAA* that the association's policies banning athletes from using their own names, images, and likenesses in video games, live game telecasts, and the like are unreasonable restraints on trade. This was a powerful blow to the NCAA's strong stance that its restrictions on student-athlete compensation are necessary to uphold its educational mission and to promote amateurism. The decision did not change the rules that prohibit players from being paid for commercial endorsements, but it does appear to open the door for them to be paid for their efforts on the field.

The *O'Bannon* opinion is no doubt only the beginning in what will be a long line of litigation and appeals in this constantly evolving relationship between players, universities, athletic departments, spectators, and professional sports teams. Nothing remains the same, and the resilient cosmos of college football, being no exception, will somehow adapt to the new regime, whatever it becomes.

Index

Index

Index

Spectators
    duty of care to, 89
    issues with, vii
    property destruction by, 95
    sovereign immunity and, 95

T

Television, 109, 110, 115
"The Wave" shrimp on a stick, 37
"Throw the Pigskin" grilled pork
    sandwiches, 86
"Time Out" hot cheese dip, 31
"Touchdown Time" chicken wings, 69

U

Uniforms, 129
University
    as employer, 27
    coach employment
        contracts with, 49, 65

    duty of care of, to players,
        5–6
    duty of care of, to spectators,
        89
    sovereign immunity of, 65,
        95
University of Alabama, 65
University of Arizona, 107
University of Kansas, 21
University of Notre Dame, 89, 121
University of Oklahoma, 115
University of San Diego, 59
University of Tennessee, 41
University of Texas, 95

V

Vanderbilt University, 49

W

Workers' compensation, 27

About the Author

Cecil C. Kuhne III is a litigator in the Dallas office of Fulbright & Jaworski L.L.P. It would be nice if he could say he was a tight end at a top-ten powerhouse before his promising career was cut short by tragic injury. However, the truth is slightly less dramatic—the only pass he ever completed was when someone threw him the barbeque sauce at a tailgate party, and the only time he came close to injury was when he dispensed too much lighter fluid at said gathering.